TOGETHER
FOR MISSION

TOGETHER FOR MISSION

*A Spiritual Commentary
on the Constitutions
of the Society of Jesus*

André de Jaer, S.J.

translated by
Francis C. Brennan, S.J.

THE INSTITUTE OF JESUIT SOURCES
Saint Louis

Number 18 in Series II: Modern Scholarly Studies
about the Society of Jesus
in English Translations

© 2001   The Institute of Jesuit Sources
3601 Lindell Boulevard
St. Louis, MO 63108

tel: [314] 977-7257
fax: [314] 977-7263
e-mail: IJS@SLU.EDU

Library of Congress Card Catalog Number: 2001086292
ISBN: 1-880810-41-7

CONTENTS

AUTHOR'S PREFACE

This book represents an effort to provide a spiritually insightful or "sapientielle" reading of the *Constitutions of the Society of Jesus*. In his 1991 letter concerning the tertianship, Fr. General Peter-Hans Kolvenbach recommended this approach for the school of the heart (*école du coeur*), which is considered the last step in the formation of a Jesuit prior to his definitive incorporation into the body of the Society of Jesus (see *Constitutions of the Society of Jesus*, no. 516).

The general viewpoint in these pages owes much to Fr. Dominique Bertrand and to the instructions on the Constitutions that between 1978 and 1984 he gave the tertians of the Province of Southern Belgium at Trosly-Breuil in France. Certain writings of Fr. Simon Decloux concerning formation have also proved invaluable. My heartfelt thanks to both of them and to numerous other authors, several of whom I have cited in the bibliography and in the footnotes throughout this book. Before my mind's eye now are the faces of the many Jesuit companions coming from almost every part of the world with whom I lived through their tertianship experience. Without them this effort would not have been possible. My gratitude goes out to all of them, as well as to the Arche community of Jean Vanier, who welcomed us with such warm friendship during the nearly twenty years we have spent in a mutual sharing of our charisms. It was revealing and stimulating to reread our own Constitutions while surrounded by this emerging community that was itself searching for the kind of written expression that would give life and body to its own spirit.

As already noted, the chapters published here are based on the author's presentation of the Constitutions to his fellow Jesuit priests and brothers making their tertianship, or third year of probation. Since the method chosen consisted in a common reading followed by discussion, a direct and informal style has been retained here, using the pronoun "we" rather than a more impersonal manner of speech. This "we" can help even the non-Jesuit reader enter into that spiritual, existential reading of the Constitutions that we are here proposing.

This work lays no claim to originality. Its aim is to help all those who would like to learn more about the spiritual path set down in the Constitutions that Ignatius, along with the First Companions, "made," as he liked to say. In the process he was from the beginning enlightened by actual, lived experience, especially during the entire sixteen years that he served as superior general. A profitable reading of these chapters would presuppose regularly referring both to the Constitutions themselves and to the Complementary Norms. This book is written in response to requests by the provincials of Madagascar and Western Africa as well as by Fr. Dideberg, provincial of Southern Belgium.

In these pages, numbers alone within parentheses will refer to **boldface** bracketed ([ ]) numbers at the left margin of the text of the *Constitutions*, while references to other sources will be designated by appropriate abbreviations. All English citations and quotations from both the Constitutions *(Cons.)* and the Complementary Norms *(CN)* will be taken from *The Constitutions of the Society of Jesus and Their Complementary Norms* (St. Louis: Institute of Jesuit Sources, 1996). Quotations and references from the memoirs of St. Ignatius are from *A Pilgrim's Testament (PilgTest)*, trans. Parmananda R. Divarkar (St. Louis: The Institute of Jesuit Sources, 1995). Quotations or references to the *Exercises* are from *The Spiritual Exercises of Saint Ignatius (SpEx)*, trans. with commentary by George E Ganss, S.J. (St. Louis: The Institute of Jesuit Sources, 1992).

Abbreviations

CN:	*Complementary Norms*
Cons.:	*The Constitutions of the Society of Jesus*
FI:	*Formula of the Institute of the Society of Jesus*
GC:	General Congregation of the Society of Jesus
GenEx:	"General Examen"
PilgTest:	*A Pilgrims's Testament: The Memoirs of Saint Ignatius of Loyola*
SpEx:	*Spiritual Exercises of St. Ignatius of Loyola*
SpirJour:	*The Spiritual Journal of St. Ignatius of Loyola*

Conventions

A number in parenthesis in this book usually refers to a **bold-faced** number at the left margin of passages in the *Constitutions of the Society of Jesus;* thus (24) indicates "paragraph" number 24 (found on page 28 of the *Constitutions*).

Similarly, (381:2) indicates the text at superscript number 2 following **bold-faced** marginal number 381 in the *Constitutions of the Society of Jesus* (found on page 160 of that book).

Similarly, (*CN* 24) indicates the bold-faced number at the left margin of passages in the *Complementary Norms;* thus (*CN* 24) indicates "paragraph" number 24 (found on page 71 of that book).

INTRODUCTION

The Objective of This Study

Whenever the spirituality of the Society of Jesus is mentioned, one thinks immediately of the Spiritual Exercises. The Exercises continue to carry a powerful gospel message for our own time; they can cause some discomfort by pressing us to confront the gospel challenge. On the other hand, even though we acknowledge that the Constitutions are clearly necessary, we do not see them as penetrating all that deeply into the heart of our vocation or of our relationship with the Holy Spirit.

We think of the Constitutions as primarily a law book having little to do with the spiritual life. At best, they blend the law with spiritual doctrine and are useful primarily for superiors as they establish policies and provide directives. The book is, however, of minimal ongoing interest to the Jesuit engaged in the apostolate. Well tested as a restraint, a protective barrier, and a last resort, the Constitutions, when viewed as a printed text and the basis of an institution, seem to act like a brake on our freedom of spirit. But as a matter of fact, as will become clearer in the course of this book, the Constitutions are a spiritual volume meriting as much attention as the Exercises. Far more than the Exercises, the Constitutions define the Jesuits and tells them who they are. For although the Exercises points out a path open to all human beings who choose to direct their lives toward God, they do not specifically define the identity of the Jesuit. What the Constitutions propose and describe is that way of proceeding toward God which is uniquely the way of the Society of Jesus.

Besides, rather then dwelling on the classical tension between the spirit and the letter, we can with good reason recognize that the ability to compose a good text and the ability to read it well are both gifts of the Spirit.[1] Hence, it is faith that has a role to play in our study of the Constitutions—an act of faith in God speaking within us through human language.

That the Church has approved the Constitutions as a way to live out the message of the Gospels and as a path to God (FI 1) guarantees that in reading and studying them we are listening to the voice of the Holy Spirit.[2] Allowing ourselves to learn from the Constitutions is a way of disposing ourselves to hear the Holy Spirit, who also approaches us through the magisterium of the Church, which has confirmed and approved this text. In this light we recognize the Constitutions as a gift that God has presented to his Church.[3] They are the outward expression of what is offered and what gives life to the Society of Jesus in and for the Church.

Reasons for Undertaking This Kind of Study

There are many reason for engaging in a reflection of this kind, especially in view of the Thirty-fourth General Congregation. The General has summoned us to it on a number of occasions: he would like to infuse a living spirit into the Constitutions comparable to what has energized the Spiritual Exercises during the past thirty years. This renewal of interest in studying the Constitutions has already manifested itself in the

---

[1] Introductory Discourses of Fr. General, no. 3, "On Our Law and Our Life," in Documents of the Thirty-Fourth General Congregation of the Society of Jesus (St. Louis: Institute of Jesuit Sources, 1995), 275–90.

[2] Exposcit debitum, no. 1:4 (p. 4). This document is the later, revised version of Regimini militantis Ecclesiæ; together they constitute the "Formula of the Institute" (FI). The citations from the "Formula" given in this book can conveniently be found in The Constitutions of the Society of Jesus and Their Complementary Norms (St. Louis: Institute of Jesuit Sources, 1996), already mentioned in the preface. As stated earlier, citations from the Constitutions (Cons.) and the Complementary Norms (CN) will also be found in this volume. In modern editions of the "Formula" and the Constitutions, the boldface numbers are subdivided into "verses" for easier reference. These references are here designated as they are in the Scriptures, that is, by "chapter" and "verse." Thus, Exposcit debitum, no. 1:4 indicates boldface number 1, verse 4. Also see the Author's Preface above.

[3] "Lumen gentium" (Dogmatic Constitution on the Church), in The Documents of Vatican II, ed. Walter M. Abbott, S.J. (New York: Guild Press, America Press, Association Press, 1966), no. 43 (p. 73).

various centers of Ignatian spirituality around the world: in France, Spain, Italy, the United States, India, [Belgium], and elsewhere. This grows out of Jesuits' profound need to understand their identity in the midst of all that is happening by way of innovation and renewal in today's Church. In addition, Vatican II called upon each religious order and congregation to return to its own original charism, and to rewrite its constitutions after a period of experimentation concluding with the promulgation of the new Code of Canon Law. For the Jesuits, this return to their origins was less a return to the Exercises than to the Constitutions. The work of revision culminated in the volume published after the Thirty-fourth General Congregation entitled *The Constitutions of the Society of Jesus and Their Complementary Norms,* already referred to earlier in this book. As the General pointed out, however, "[T]hese revised and newly published *Constitutions* will remain a dead letter, little more than a treasure to be preserved in the archives, unless we dedicate ourselves to studying them and putting them into practice in our daily lives as Jesuits propelled by the same enthusiasm that we have for the *Exercises.*"

> It is important, in this connection, to recall that St. Ignatius gave at least as much time and attention to the composition of the Constitutions as he did to revising and editing the Exercises. This involved an extraordinary amount of work beginning in 1539 with the "Deliberation of the First Fathers" and left uncompleted at the time of his death in 1556.[4]

We know how careful St. Ignatius was throughout this long process faithfully to transmit the experience of the First Companions. We have not received in the Constitutions an ancient text meant to be preserved as a relic. Nor do we have here merely a rule book, although this volume does contain a certain number of juridical norms. Through contemplating the Constitutions, we are invited to involve ourselves in a way of proceeding (547:7) that will enable us to continue founding the Society of Jesus in response to the Holy Spirit and with a fidelity that is both creative and firmly rooted in the Church. In the Constitutions we encounter a spiritual work that calls for a

---

[4] André Ravier, *Ignatius of Loyola and the Founding of the Society of Jesus* (San Francisco: Ignatius Press, 1987), 230–67.

spiritual reading, that is, a reading guided by the light of the Holy Spirit. Consequently, our presentation of the Constitutions in the following chapters does not envision a technical study, but rather a Spirit-infused reading ("de type sapientiel"), as suggested by Fr. General in his 1991 letter on the tertianship. This kind of reading

> strives to assimilate the insight, the inspiration, and the challenge which the texts can provide for the life of the individual and of the Society as a whole. It introduces into the group consciousness certain reactions and reflections occasioned in each individual by intimate contact with these documents of an essentially existential character.[5]

For this reason, it is good to recall how the Constitutions were composed, in order to understand better how this book is to be read.

How Were the Constitutions Written?

We do not plan to rehearse in detail the busy life led by Ignatius during the same period in which he drafted the Constitutions.[6] Suffice it to note that he governed the nascent Society, directed numerous novices, carried on a varied apostolate in the city of Rome, was a spiritual advisor much in demand, carried on an immense correspondence—all this despite many months of chronic illness.

In the last paragraphs of his *Pilgrim's Testament,* Ignatius himself explains how he "made the Constitutions." Let it suffice to quote one passage: "The method which he followed while he was drafting the Constitutions was to say Mass each day, to present to God the point that he was treating, and to pray over it; he always had tears at prayer and Mass."[7] The extant fragments from Ignatius's *Spiritual Journal* reveal him at work on the Constitutions at a very precise and crucial point:

---

[5] *Acta Romana* 20, no. 4 (1992): 629.

[6] Ravier, *Ignatius,* 321–89.

[7] *A Pilgrim's Testament: Memoirs of St. Ignatius of Loyola (PilgTest),* trans. Parmananda R. Divarkar, S.J. (St. Louis: Institute of Jesuit Sources, 1995), no. 101 (p. 149).

deciding on the poverty to be observed by the Society's churches.

If we permit ourselves to be guided by Ignatius's own written records and by what his secretary Polanco tells us concerning the manner in which Ignatius worked on the Constitutions, we establish definitively that these texts grew out of experience, enhanced by thoughtful discernment, deep reflection, and constant prayer.[8] The Constitutions reflect the experiences lived by the First Companions while they were laying the foundation of the Society.[9] They also represent the later experiences of those companions who joined the Society in the years right after its foundation (see 211, 220, 414, 624).

Furthermore, in its basic layout the Constitutions do not amount to a theoretical disquisition governed by abstract logic. Instead, they carefully follow the experience of an individual who is called by God to join the Society, and they conduct him through his progressive incorporation. That is to say, the same topics, such as poverty, obedience, and the spiritual life, will recur even at the risk of wearying the spirits of those who are too rigidly logical or juridical.[10] The dynamic invariably takes the form of a process based on experience, analogous to what is operative in the Spiritual Exercises with its movement toward personal conversion.

At the same time, this experience is not transmitted in an unrefined, blunt state. It has been subjected to much thought and analysis over a period long enough to allow for clear and lasting distinctions between what really proceeds from God and his action in founding the Society and what proceeds from merely human trial and error. That is why Ignatius was so careful to place before the Lord in prayer and at Mass each morning all the issues to be dealt with in the Constitutions. He did not cast these matters in their final form until he had obtained confirmation from God, an interior assurance that a given point was in harmony with the mission God had entrusted to the Society and also with that way of living the

---

[8] Ravier, *Ignatius of Loyola,* 252–61.

[9] *FI* 7 (p. 10); see also *Cons.* 81, 605.

[10] Regarding Bobadilla, see Ravier, *Ignatius,* 248 and 267.

Gospels marked out by God. But there again, Ignatius did not hesitate to revise and correct anew in the light of experience, of events, and of historical developments. That was his practice until death came for him. Thus did Ignatius cooperate with the action of God, who was founding the Society and wished to sustain and develop it down through the centuries (see 812). God's share in the work was his wisdom and benevolence in the act of founding the Society (134), while the human response was a continuing effort to seek out the divine will (134, 414, 812, etc.)

How to Read the Constitutions

Our approach to reading the Constitutions parallels the manner in which Ignatius "made" this text. He intended it to be read and applied as a work of spiritual discernment. It helps us, as followers and successors of St. Ignatius, to discern in our own concrete historical situation just how the Lord desires us to cooperate in the work that he wishes to go on accomplishing through the Society. The Constitutions do not tell us specifically what needs to be done: they do not function primarily as a law book. What they do above all is provide sound criteria for reflection and judgment leading to action. They are a help toward making an election and reaching decisions. They afford us the opportunity to shed light on current questions by subjecting them to the criteria found in the Constitutions and by placing everything before God in the prayer that seeks to discover what he wills.

Given that the Constitutions were "made" in accordance with the spiritual experience lived and discerned by Ignatius and the First Companions, it is essential to know and be familiar with that experience if we hope to read the Constitutions in accord with their original purpose and function. This experience is recalled for us in the writings left to us by Master Ignatius. The two principal sources are, first of all, the *Spiritual Exercises* and, second, the *Pilgrim's Testament*. The *Spiritual Exercises* holds the key to the evangelical experience and to the manner of proceeding proper to Ignatius and his first companions: the attachment to the poor and humble Christ of the Kingdom and the Two Standards—the Christ who calls us and sends us to help souls and to search and find in the light of this call whatever is God's will for our lives. As to the *Testament,* Nadal states that it describes one way of founding the Society.[11] "Ignatius did not wish to talk about himself; he did not transmit an autobiography but rather a testament including from his own life only what might be helpful for the companions at all times and in all places."[12] This principle had already governed his composition of the Exercises (*PilgTest* 99). To these two principal writings should be added another two whose importance cannot be overemphasized. The *Spiritual Journal* portrays Ignatius concentrating intensely on one single but critical provision of the Constitutions, while also revealing the mystical and Eucharistic dimension of his work of composition. Finally, there are the Letters, in which the spiritual master concretely applied the lessons of the Exercises and the Constitutions to a wide variety of actual situations.

Stages in the Composition of the Formula of the Institute and the Constitutions

The table in the box on page 10 contains the principal dates for the gradual composition of the Constitutions. In the book we have already cited, Fr. Ravier described in some detail this long process of formation.[13] For his own part, Dominique Bertrand likewise describes this slow development and analyzes the meaning of these stages and the extended editorial process involved.[14] Without embarking on a complex study of these matters, we merely remark how the Constitutions were "made" with a constant effort to listen to lived experience carefully and discerningly. Ignatius never wished to be considered the actual author of the Constitutions, but rather "the one among us charged with composing it"; and he was careful to have the First Companions critique and correct what he wrote. It happened as a result of these gradual stages that two founding

---

[11] Luis Gonçalves, S.J., *Le Récit du pélerin: Autobiographie de saint Ignace de Loyola,* trans. A. Lauras, notes by J.-Cl. Dhôtel, Christus Collection (Paris: Desclée De Brouwer, 1988), p. 53, no. 4.

[12] Ibid., 40.

[13] *Ignatius,* 229–52.

[14] Dominique Bertrand, *Un Corps pour l'Esprit: Essai sur les Constitutions,* Christus Collection, no. 38 (Paris: Desclée De Brouwer, 1974), 45–53.

documents took shape only over a period of time—the Formula of the Institute, that is, in its two versions of 1540 and 1550, as well as the Constitutions itself.

The Formula of the Institute is the text specifically approved by the Pope in the bull formally establishing the Society.[15] It is the document that gives us our identity. There the companions set forth the essence of the life plan that they received as a grace to be lived out in the Church and in the world (*CN* 20, §1). Everything is already there in summary version: the purpose of the Society along with the basic means for implementing the plan. Without the approval of the Holy See, this Formula cannot be changed, not even by a general congregation (*CN* 21, §1).

The Constitutions along with the General Examen detail the path to be followed in implementing and living out the Formula. It does not simply constitute a later commentary on the earlier text. Rather, it is designed as the path to be discovered anew by each companion as he puts into practice the charism of the Society, to be received in the grace given us, as expressed in the Formula. The Constitutions and the General Examen aid us to proceed better, in conformity with our Institute, along the path of divine service on which we have entered (134). Just as the Formula of the Institute gives us our identity, so the Constitutions are designed to enhance our comprehension and *understanding* of that identity. It defines the stages by which each person called by God to the Society is gradually united to it, and also the stages in the development of the entire group.

For their part, the general congregations, through legislative activity proper to each historical period, speak to us more about what must be done at a specific moment in history. They are there to promote the actual *exercise* of our identity and our apostolic works.

---

[15] *Complementary Norms*, 9, §1. The text of the *Constitutions (Cons.)* and the *Complementary Norms (CN)* will be found in the volume cited in n. 2 above.

The Work of the Thirty-Fourth General Congregation

GC 34 undertook to restore the original impact of the Constitutions, which were intended to be both inspirational and at the same time normative for the life of the Society. To that end, the congregation took note of those elements in the text no longer applicable today, and also modified any other points that required updating in light of current circumstances. As a result of their work, the Constitutions remain a privileged expression of the original spiritual and apostolic experience of the First Companions, while retaining a central and living place in our own actual lives. To its latest edition of the Constitutions, the congregation has added the Complementary Norms, gathering together whatever specifies more clearly our vocation and our mission today, in light of the history of the Society and especially through the contributions of the more recent congregations. A fuller explanation of this project will be found in Fr. Kolvenbach's preface to this new edition (pp. xi to xiv) and in the first five complementary norms (*CN* 1–5).

In an article published in *Manresa*, Fr. Iglesias clarifies the relationship between the Complementary Norms and the Constitutions.[16] The Norms constitute the sign and the practical results introduced by the Constitutions into our "manner of proceeding," and they provide criteria for discernment that presuppose an attitude of creative fidelity on our part. Ignatius never wanted to bring the Constitutions to completion; on the contrary, he left them open to the future, as Part X clearly shows. That is why the Complementary Norms are not designed to be the last word, but as a moment in the process of cooperation ever open to the work that God wills to accomplish through "this least Society of Jesus."

---

[16] Ignatio Iglesias, "Constitutiones para hacer Constitutiones," *Manresa* 70 (1997): 165–69.

STAGES IN THE FOUNDATION OF THE SOCIETY OF JESUS AND THE DEVELOPMENT OF THE INSTITUTE

ORGANIZATION: THE FIRST COMPANIONS WORK TOGETHER

Aug. 15, 1534	Vows at Montmartre; the first community decision
June 24, 1537	Ordinations to the priesthood
Sept. 1537	Venice: Decision to be called by the name of Jesus.
Nov. 1537	Arrival in Rome; Vision at La Storta
Nov. 1538	The offer to the Pope; the First Mass of Ignatius on Christmas, 1538
Spring 1539	Deliberation of the First Fathers, 1539
Apr. 15, 1539	Solemn pledge to make a vow of obedience if approved by the Pope
Apr.–June 1539	The deliberations continue; first effort to clarify the plan of life
Jul.–Aug. 1539	Composition of the "Five Chapters"
Sept. 3, 1539	The Pope orally approves the "Five Chapters"
Sept. 27, 1540	The Pope gives written approval to the first version of the "Formula": *Regimini militantis Ecclesiæ*
Apr. 8–19, 1541	Difficult election of the superior general
Apr. 22, 1541	The Society offered up to God: profession of the First Companions at St. Paul's outside the Walls

PERIOD OF EXPERIMENTATION: IGNATIUS WORKS ALONE ON THE *CONSTITUTIONS*

1541	First attempt at certain constitutions: poverty
1541–1546	They ward off harassment and answer questions presented
1544	*Spiritual Journal*
1546	First Version of the "General Examen," to answer questions and provide criteria for accepting postulants; origin of the grade of coadjutors

PERIOD OF FORMULATION: IGNATIUS AND POLANCO TOGETHER; DEVELOPMENT OF THE TEXT

1547	Polanco arrives in Rome; groundbreaking; review of other religious orders and their rules
1548	Papal approval of the *Spiritual Exercises* 1549–1550 First complete text of the Constitutions: "text *a*" →

1550	Formula of the Institute, second version: *Exposcit debitum*
1550–1551	The *Constitutions,* text *A*
1551–1556	Text *B:* text *A* + notes by Ignatius = autograph text
1558	Text *C:* text *B* (except for certain variants) translated into Latin and approved in Rome by GC 1
1590	Text *D* (Spanish) approved by the GC 5 with a few variants of text *C*

PREAMBLE TO THE CONSTITUTIONS

PLAN

Why "make" constitutions? (134)
How to make the *Constitutions* (135)
Purpose of the *Constitutions* and the role of the *Declarations* (136)
The order of the ten parts (137)

STRUCTURE OF NO. 134

Although	God our Creator and Lord is the one who in his Supreme Wisdom and Goodness must preserve, direct, and carry forward in his divine service this least Society of Jesus,
And although	on our own part, what helps most toward this end must be, more than any exterior constitution, the interior law of charity and love which the Holy Spirit writes and imprints upon hearts;
Nevertheless	since . . . since. . . and since,

We think it necessary that constitutions should be written to help us. . . .

PLAN OF THE *CONSTITUTIONS* (137)

From the less complete it proceeds by stages toward the completion of what must be accomplished. Each part will prescribe one stage which will also contribute a substantial and permanent feature to our lives.

Examen: The background of our vocation: school of the heart
Prologue: The beginning, which is ever present
Parts I and II: Vocation and first admission

    I. Permanence of the yes pronounced by me and by the Society

    II. Permanence of the no, which was not pronounced in my case

Parts III and IV: Formation

    III. In virtue and the spiritual life

    IV. In knowledge

Parts V and VI: Incorporation

    V. The candidate is joined to the body of the Society

    VI. And lives until death as a member

Part VII: Sent on Mission

Parts VIII and IX: Responsibility for the group

    VIII. Union of the group

    IX. Government of the group

Part X: Preservation and increase of the entire group

THE PREAMBLE TO THE CONSTITUTIONS (134–137)

One way of undertaking a spiritually insightful reading of the Preamble is to pay close attention to the theme of beginning. Master Ignatius attaches considerable importance to beginnings. We have only to recall the significance of the preludes to his meditations. Often he himself was constrained to begin all over again, for example, when he was not permitted to remain in the Holy Land (*PilgTest* 50). There is a mystery in beginning and in beginning anew. For Ignatius it always involves a deferring to God and a breaking-through to what is actually real in any situation. The tertianship is one of those times when we begin anew, starting from God and at ground level. Our whole life is, in fact, a series of new beginnings: only by beginning over again can we really continue at all. We have not found a good way to be a Jesuit if we continue in that life simply because that is what we have done until now. I cannot actually be a Jesuit except by starting off again today, starting from God. "Every day I begin." Just by adverting to the textual history of this Preamble, we are able to recognize the wisdom, fortified through the years, with which Ignatius begins his Constitutions.

TEXTUAL HISTORY AND ARRANGEMENT OF THE PREAMBLE

Nos. 136 and 137 are included in the versions *a* and *A* of 1550 (consult the outline, p. 11, of the stages in the composition of the Constitutions), whereas nos. 134 and 135 appear only in text *B* of 1556, where they are placed at the beginning of the Preamble. It is a revealing clue to the way in which Ignatius worked, always starting from life as it is, from concrete experience, and from a sense of what is actually necessary, namely, the need for written constitutions; then he had to determine what shape to give them, how to distinguish those points that are more fundamental and universal from those that are more specific and detailed, how in the end to work out their orderly arrangement. These questions led to the composition of nos. 136 and 137 in 1550.

Then between 1550 and 1556 Ignatius continues to pray and to improve the text, eventually situating it more logically within his overall vision of God's design (134) and imparting to it an organic, developmental structure (135). As a result, the text that most clearly explains the rationale for the Constitutions were written at the very end of the editorial process, then placed at the beginning of the completed work. This demonstrates how the Constitutions are something of an afterthought, the fruit of experiences first lived and then refined and clarified before God. The actual experience of the First Companions precedes the written Constitutions, while the action of God precedes the actual founding of the Society. Only gradually could they offer a rationale for what they were living, explain it, and give it written expression. It is in the Preamble, then, that we have a clear indication of how the Constitutions came to be and how they must be read and understood.

ANALYSIS OF THE TEXT

Why Write Constitutions? (134)

In his preface to the Spanish commentary on the Constitutions—a commentary directed to the "average" Jesuit *(Jesuita medio)*—Fr. Kolvenbach presents this introductory text in the Constitutions in a very thought-provoking way. According to him, this Preamble reveals, in its own way, that the Constitutions themselves are addressed to the plain, ordinary, "average" reality of every Jesuit.[1] In effect, Ignatius explains in this text just why he began to compose the Constitutions. His point of

---

[1] See S. Arzubialde, ed., *Constitutiones de la Compañía de Jesús* (Bilbao: Mensajero-Sal Terrae, 1994), 8.

departure is the basic attitudes common to the average Jesuit. In the first place, we have the Jesuit's confidence in the wisdom and goodness of God, who alone can "preserve, direct, and carry forward in his divine service this least Society of Jesus just as he deigned to begin it." In the second place, he presumes the Jesuit's deep conviction that obedience to the Holy Spirit and to his interior guidance, conformed to "the interior law of charity and love," is much more decisive than any constitutions in securing his fidelity to God. Having thus established the relative importance of constitutions and once again addressing the average Jesuit, Ignatius goes on to highlight the necessity for constitutions and their meaning. He points out that this volume exemplifies the cooperation of the creature with the action of the Creator, and views its composition as an act of obedience to the Vicar of Christ and in conformity with the demands of reason and the example of the saints. This is how the Constitutions address the average Jesuit, who is at one and the same time wholly centered on God and actively immersed in the Christian history of salvation. In this way, such a Jesuit will be able to read the Constitutions and be enlightened by it, so that he can the better understand the grace that he has received and learn how to cooperate with it. This approach to the Constitutions is "sapientielle" or spiritually oriented rather than technical or scholarly. Thus, its aim, in accord with Fr. Kolvenbach's suggestion, is to enlighten and point out the way.

Here follow some guidelines to help the reader understand the Preamble and make it a part of himself.

▸ The text is constructed in the form of an election of the third time, as shown in the outline on page 12. Reasons that seem at first to make it useless to write constitutions are followed by the more positive considerations that lead to the conclusion that "constitutions should be written to help us proceed better."

▸ The text embodies a theocentric vision: it evokes God's entire plan, with its Trinitarian movement and broad theological perspective. For Ignatius and his companions one thing is clear: God is at the origin of this least Society of Jesus; he it is who still governs it today, and he is the one who will cause it to advance in his service.

▸ It emphasizes the interior law of charity and love that the Holy Spirit impresses upon hearts. Ignatius will often return to this point, that it is the Holy Spirit who will enable us to discern what is proper (219, 414, 624). And he underscores this first of all in those situations where it is difficult to maintain the primacy of love, for example, in dismissing (218–30) or in punishing someone (270).

▸ The movement of this text also reveals an incarnational dynamic that is typical of Ignatian thought. It begins with an opening to the mystery of God and to the love that the Holy Spirit implants in our hearts—a love that humbly embodies itself in the darkness of the real world and freely limits itself within the structures required for the life of the body. This same dynamic is found in the key meditations of the Exercises, such as the Incarnation and the Kingdom.

▸ The priority given to the action of God in the existence and the ongoing life of the Society is thus total. At the same time, the necessity of human cooperation, far from being excluded, is emphatically called for. This same paradox will appear again at the conclusion of the Constitutions (812 and 814).

▸ The Constitutions are intended to *assist* us to "proceed better in conformity with our Institute along the path of divine service on which we have entered" (134). To assist: there we have a salient characteristic of the Ignatian style. His primary concern is not to compel but rather to invite others to enter in total freedom on a path that leads to God through following Christ in the Society. Along this path the Constitutions will provide light and direction.

How to Write the Constitutions? (135)

Following a logical order, the Formula of the Institute commenced by stating the purpose of the Society and then went on to briefly sketch means for achieving it. The plan chosen by Ignatius for the Constitutions, however, moves in the opposite direction, developmentally. The Constitutions follow each stage in the life of a companion as he is progressively assimilated into the apostolic body of the Society and its mission. What we have, therefore, is a kind of missionary journey that faithfully and in a very original way traces the actual experience of the First Companions. As Fr. André Ravier has somewhat playfully remarked, "The 'ontogeny' of each companion reproduced the 'phylogeny' of the Society."[2]

THE PURPOSE AND FUNCTION OF THE DECLARATIONS (136)

The first draft of the Constitutions begins with this no. 136, stating its purpose and the needs that it is intended to meet. There follows an explanation of the Declarations, which are printed in italics and seek to nuance with greater precision the more universal and fundamental provisions of the Constitutions. The Declarations, which impart a certain flexibility to their counterpart, are one more sign that the Constitutions are not primarily a book that tells us what to do, but rather a work designed to help us discern what needs to be done.

Hence the Constitutions do not represent the complete legislative legacy of the Society. They do not supplant the general congregations, and especially not the Complementary Norms issued by GC 34 (*CN* 5, §1). But all these more contemporary documents must be set in place and applied in the light of the Constitutions (*CN* 5, §2).

The Order of the Constitutions and Its Significance (137)

This declaration recalls no. 135, which states the developmental concept behind the organization of the Constitutions. Each Part will develop a given stage on our journey as companions of Jesus, a specific period in our gradual incorporation into the Society and its mission. Reflecting on this structure, we readily perceive that the different parts are so organized as to reflect the lived experience of individual Jesuits.

▸ General Examen: One knocks at the door of the Society; prelude to a vocation.

---

[2] *Ignatius*, 252.

- ‣ Prologue: The beginning, which always remains present.
- ‣ Parts I and II: The vocation, which is either confirmed or not.

    Permanence of the "yes" pronounced by me and by the Society.

    Permanence of a "no," which was not, in fact, uttered.

- ‣ Parts III and IV: Formation in it that is spiritual (III) and academic (IV).
- ‣ Parts V and VI: Termination in definitive incorporation.

    One becomes a member of the group in a specific grade.

    One lives until death as a man of God in this Society.

- ‣ Part VII: One is sent into the vineyard of Christ our Lord.
- ‣ Parts VIII and IX: Responsibility for the group.

    Part VIII: Concerning the union of the members with one another and with the head.

    Part IX: One is governed and motivated within the group.

- ‣ Part X: One watches over the preservation and development of the group.

It is essential to carefully note the actual developmental stage described in each Part of the Constitutions in order fully to grasp what is said there. Something said in Part III, which is mostly about novices, will carry a meaning quite different from the same thing said in Part VI, which treats of the formed Jesuit working in the apostolate. As we will see, it is not appropriate to speak in the same way about poverty, obedience, or the spiritual life when talking about different stages in Jesuit life. Nevertheless, nothing is to be considered outdated or discarded. The different stages are melded and integrated; and each Part of the Constitutions, while treating a specific stage, will also contribute a permanent dimension that should remain throughout our lives. The Jesuit cannot know himself without including his whole past in the present. It is especially good, particularly during the tertianship, to reflect on the journey from its very beginning up to now, not in order to count up the scars of old battles, but rather to rediscover the qualities of one's own Jesuit self. Reading the Constitutions puts me in touch with everything that contributes to my present identity and my fidelity. There is a sense in which I enter the Society every day: "Today I begin." That approach helps me to shed a lifeless notion of vocation—something a little tired and weary, perhaps used up and weighed down by the years—and to rekindle an attitude toward vocation as a fresh, energy-imparting election for today.

KEY CONCEPTS THAT ASSIST THE READER TO ENTER UPON THE PATH OF THE *CONSTITUTIONS*

To build up a group for God: the theocentric character of the *Constitutions*
  For the service (167 times), the praise, the glory (151 times) of God through help for souls;
    rooted in the experience of the Exercises: 23, 46, 169, 179, 184;
    the basic criterion being service: the standard of Christ, calling for humble servants and poor: 146, 147, 167, 97.
  So that God may be served by this body:
    The Society: an instrument at the disposal of God to do his work; docile in the hands of God; "in the Lord" (400 times).
    Rooted in the Exercises: to seek and to find God's will by following in the path of Christ.
An apostolic purpose: always there: "to help souls, to assist the neighbor"
The preeminence of grace, calling on human endeavor
Continual discernment: the medium through which an ongoing dynamic of election is active
The pivotal role of the Church and of the Roman Pontiff in the body of the Society and in its missions
Obedience in undertaking the mission: a unifying element imparting a sense of apostolic commitment to each companion
The principle of reality: Continual sensitivity to circumstances and to differences among persons, places, backgrounds, as well as historical and cultural situations and conditions
Concern for the poor and the lowly; to preach in poverty and to serve the faith in promoting justice
Willingness to live and work in the midst of creative tensions
  The Ignatian dialectic of inclusion rather than opposition
  Confidence in God alone and cultivation of human skills; priests along with brothers
  Professed along with coadjutors; the poor along with the well educated; freedom and obedience; indifference but also total commitment; preference for the poor and the young along with a presence among the more responsible; dispersed and yet united; contemplative in action
  Spiritual apostolate and promotion of justice; mobility and stability

Examen: Marks of a Vocation to the Society of Jesus (1–133)

A. General Examen

Chap. 1: The features distinguishing the Society from other orders are explained to the candidate (I–21).

The purpose of the Institute (1–3)

Means to achieve this purpose: the evangelical counsels (4–6); the vow of obedience to the pope (7); manner of life (8–9); diversity of membership (10–15); prolonged period of probation (16–21)

Chaps. 2 & 3: Questions to ascertain the candidate's vocation (22–52)

Chap. 2: The impediments (22–29); unnecessary to proceed further if impediments are identified (30–32)

Chap. 3: Positive information concerning the candidate (34–52): Who is he? (34–35); his family (36–39); the circumstances of his life (40–49); his religious vocation (50); and to the Society (51)? With all this clarified, does he wish to enter? Let us proceed from there.

Chap. 4: The explanation of the most important facts needed to be known and understood by the candidate prior to entrance (53–103). See the outline of chapter 4. At each step the candidate is asked if he understands and freely accepts what is presented.

B. Special Examens

Chap. 5: For educated candidates (104–11). Note the humility demanded of everyone (111). This indicates that different sorts of persons were applying for membership in the Society.

Chap. 6: For the coadjutors alone (112–20). Concern that they be faithful, happy, and at peace in their specific calling (117–18). The brothers or temporal coadjutors "will strive in their spiritual conversations to obtain the greater good of their neighbor" (115).

Chap. 7: For the scholastics (121–29). Concern that their decision will be definitive

Chap. 8: For those still indifferent 130–133): instruction and advice "so that both sides may proceed with greater knowledge and clarity in the Lord" (133)

CHAPTER 4 OF THE *EXAMEN*

Men detached from the world and determined to serve God completely (53–63)

    renunciation of worldly possessions (53–59)

    separation from friends and family (60–62)

    self-denial with the aid of fraternal correction (63)

Experiments characteristic of our vocation (64–79)

    the Exercises (65)

    the hospital (66)

    the pilgrimage (67)

    domestic service (68)

    teaching catechism to children (69)

    preaching and hearing confessions (70)

    evaluation (71–79)

Community life in the house (80–90)

    the sacraments (80)

    poverty (81–82)

    humility and self-denial (82–83)

    obedience (84–90)

Toward complete assimilation into the Society (91–103)

    the account of conscience (91–97)

    incorporation into the Society (98–100)

    the attachment of one's whole being to Christ poor, humble, and scorned (101–3)

THE FIRST AND GENERAL
EXAMEN (1–133)

ORIGIN AND PURPOSE OF THE EXAMEN

I n 1540, when the Society was founded and approved by Pope Paul III, a number of helpful friends had already gathered around the First Companions, wishing to collaborate with them. These associates included priests, lay people of various ages and occupations, educated persons, simple folk, and so forth. They were attracted by the apostolic energy and enthusiasm of the companions, and some of them hoped to be more closely connected to the group in ways suited to their qualifications. By 1540, Ignatius had decided to accept a certain number of young students who might offer some hope of becoming good workers in the vineyard of Christ our Lord (308). For one thing, the most valued companions of Ignatius were already being sent on assignment by the Pope (Francis Xavier, Favre, Laínez, Bobadilla, and others). Although this was in accord with their primary purpose and, of course, with their vow of obedience to the Sovereign Pontiff regarding missions (605), still, Ignatius was losing his best collaborators. For these reasons, among others, the idea of admitting and incorporating helpers or coadjutors took form; these would be either priests or laymen who would not personally be bound by the vow to the pope and could therefore remain available to meet the internal needs of the new order.

It was necessary, nonetheless, that those who were to be received and associated with the Society in this way would clearly understand what kind of life they were choosing and would be able to find happiness and peace in their vocation.

This is how Ignatius came to compose the Examen bit by bit. Some rough drafts appeared from around 1540, when he conceived the idea of accepting students. But not until 1546, just as the Pope authorized the Society to receive coadjutors, did Ignatius finish composing the first complete version of the Examen. So it was written well before the first edition of the *Constitutions*, which bears the date 1550. The final redaction of the Examen was completed in 1556, but it differs from the first edition only in minor details. It had been planned originally as the fifth chapter of Part I of the Constitutions, but that idea was abandoned in favor of placing it at the beginning of the entire book. This corresponds, of course, to the developmental plan of the Constitutions, so concerned with a gradual pedagogical and spiritual progression toward integration into the body of the Society.

Thus the Examen aims to discern whether or not the person asking to enter the Society is really called by the Lord to this particular vocation in the Church. To this end, the Examen helps by promoting a clearer mutual understanding. First of all, it sets out for the candidate the characteristics that are basic to the Society; it furnishes the answer to his question, "What are you, Society of Jesus?" (chap. 1), and proceeds to describe in considerable detail the kind of life and the sort of spiritual attitudes that follow from this vocation (chap. 4). On the other hand, it provides an occasion for dialogue that in turn helps to make the candidate better known (chaps. 2 and 3) and to discern whether in fact he has a genuine vocation to the Society. These first four chapters, called the General Examen *(Gen-Ex)*, are proposed to all the candidates and are the ones we will analyze first of all. Chapters 5 to 8 are more specific examens that apply only to some candidates. The box on page 21 provides a general outline of the Examen.

A close affinity between the Examen and the Exercises is readily apparent. In effect, the Examen points out a concrete way of putting the Exercises into practice throughout one's whole life. To be sure, the path of the Constitutions is clearly delineated here, but we must not lose sight of the singularly personal way of proceeding proper to the Exercises. There is also a close connection between the Formula of the Institute and the Examen. First of all, both texts were written by Ignatius himself. He did not yet have a secretary; only later, after the arrival of Polanco in 1547, would he have such an aide during the composition of the Constitutions. Furthermore, the two texts share the same inspiration, since the Examen specifically applies to an individual candidate what is explained in general terms by the Formula.

SOME CHARACTERISTICS OF THE EXAMEN

The Examen is introduced as the *beginning of a conversation* between the Society and the candidate.[1] For Ignatius the first priority is to undertake an exchange of ideas. This reflects, of course, the emphasis he had given to spiritual conversation throughout his life; furthermore, in those days this was an entirely original way of receiving a new recruit. It is clear that Ignatius placed a high premium on mutual understanding as a help in evaluating candidates. Hence, we observe throughout the text (18, 130, 133, 34, 104, 112) a determination to proceed with *complete clarity* and sincerity in an atmosphere of openness and trust. This is a kind of invitation to take the first steps in the process of manifesting one's conscience—an activity so fundamental to the life of each companion and of the entire Society.

Equally strong is an emphasis on the *discernment of spiritual desire.* Such verbal formulas as "Does he feels it is good for him?" "Does he freely accept?" "Does he have the desire?" occur frequently (52, 57, 60, 63, 101, 133) and reveal Ignatius's strong insistence on this point. For Ignatius sought to attract recruits with "ardent desires in our Lord (101, 102), and the presence of such agreement, such desires, is evidence of whether it is the Holy Spirit at work in the candidate's request for admission.

One basic disposition is expected of the person who would enter the order, and that is *indifference*, the complete willingness to be incorporated into the Society in whatever manner may eventually be decided (10, 15, 111, 132). This indifference is rooted in a key theme of the Exercises, in the

---

[1] See nos. 31, 52, 133, and chap. 4 passim.

Principle and Foundation (*SpEx* 23), that is, and in the Third Class of Men (*SpEx* 155). Moreover, it is very important for the candidate to exhibit from the beginning a settled desire for *stability* in his vocation: "Has he a deliberate determination in the Lord to live and die with and in this Society of Jesus our Creator and Lord?" (51, and also 18, 27, 30, 116).

THE IMPORTANCE OF THE EXAMEN TODAY

This is a document that sets out the basic criteria for a vocation to the Society of Jesus. It corresponds to the first stage of the entire journey that is the future life of every companion. To be sure, a few details reflect an earlier age and are not applicable as such to the situation today. However, the volume published by GC 34 entitled *The Constitutions of the Society of Jesus and Their Complementary Norms,* cited above, clearly demonstrates that the Examen retains its original force, which is at once inspirational and normative for the Society's life. Since it often happens today that a candidate will have little or no acquaintance with the Society (and vice versa), an initial dialogue aimed at mutual understanding and conducted after the manner of the Examen and in the light of the Complementary Norms (*CN* 25–27) assumes great importance. At the same time, we should bear in mind that although it is written for the new recruit, the Examen does in fact give expression to certain permanent values in our Jesuit life. It conveys the spiritual attitudes and dispositions required if one is to live happily as a companion of Jesus. My vocation as a Jesuit is alive today to the extent that I fully embrace, relish, and love the basic attitudes described in the Examen, especially in chapter 4. Of course, it goes without saying that they will be deepened, tested, and strengthened during the years to come.

SURVEY OF CHAPTERS 1 TO 3

The *first chapter* describes the Society primarily by pointing out those characteristics that distinguish it from other religious orders: its particular purpose, the nature of its poverty and obedience—especially the vow to the Sovereign Pontiff with regard to missions—the ordinary manner of life, the different categories of its members, and the long period of formation. This description deals with externals primarily, but we must not overlook the description of the Society as "this least congregation," terminology so dear to Ignatius. If we wish to be the real Society of Jesus, we must accept the reality of its "littleness." Furthermore, it is situated from the outset within the Church, having been approved by it and placed at the pope's disposal.

Chapter 2 enumerates the impediments that would normally render entrance impossible. Should one of these be discovered in the course of these inquiries, the dialogue would not proceed further; but we take note of the Christlike compassion that Ignatius recommends in these circumstances (31, 32).

In *chapter 3* the exchange becomes increasingly more personal and more intimate. The candidate is asked to recount the major events in his life and to describe those personal experiences that influence his affective relationship with God. In this way, the conversation returns to the history of his vocation and to the maturity of his decision (50). "Does he have a well-founded determination in the Lord, formed in complete freedom, to live and die with and in this Society of Jesus our Creator and Lord?" (51). If some doubt remains, it is better to delay the admission somewhat, so that the candidate can lay the matter before the Lord "and thus be able to proceed with greater spiritual energies" (51). The examiner will verify with the candidate whether he has been able to make a decision that is deeply rooted in his own free will and the grace of God (52). If the matter is clear to both parties, they will then be able to turn to chapter 4, which penetrates to the essence of the Society's spirit.

CHAPTER 4 OF THE EXAMEN (53–103)

Exposition of Its Structure

Entrance into the Society of Jesus is a crucial turning point in a life notable for a conversion and a radical and definitive choice to follow Christ. It involves a long process, and

Ignatius asks the candidate at the outset to give careful consideration to how it all develops. The outline on page 22 maps out in broad strokes, as it were, a spiritual journey along which the candidate will be guided, one that will organize and unify his desires to follow Christ.

Anyone reading this plan is able to retrace the steps taken by St. Ignatius after his own conversion: he left Loyola and his family, underwent a spiritual rebirth at Manresa, lived in a hospital, went on pilgrimage to Jerusalem. The same kind of experience lived by the First Companions after the completion of their studies in Paris is present here in the background. The text contains explicit references to this (53, 81, 82), giving us one more indication of how these texts were written in the light of experience refined by reflection and prayer.

The Meaning and Importance of Chapter 4

Here St. Ignatius maps out the apostolic journey offered to anyone called to enter the Society, along with the spiritual and apostolic attitudes that must be fundamental to the life of a prospective member. It is by adopting these attitudes and engaging in these practices that the candidate is initiated into the life proper to our Institute. But the candidate must accept and understand all this as a gift offered by God, as a grace-filled path upon which he is invited to enter, and not as an ideal to be realized through his own personal energies alone. Hence, it is important for each candidate to know whether or not this gift is in fact being offered. And this in turn will be ascertained chiefly by considering the desire, the attraction, and the hunger for this kind of enterprise. Consequently, the document is full of pointed questions for the candidate: "Is he in agreement?" "Does he freely choose?" "Has he the desire?" (55, 57, 60, 63, 90, 98, 100, 101) "or at least the desire to desire?" (102). The exchange proceeds after the manner of an election of the second time (*SpEx* 176), attentive to the movements of the spirits. To be sure, not everything concerning the spiritual and apostolic life of a Jesuit is going to be found here in chapter 4—certainly not with the maturity and fullness found later in numbers 812–14, 582, 547, 288, and so forth. Nevertheless, these pages do constitute a solid synthesis of what is most essential to our vocation: the resolve to empty ourselves of all that keeps us from being like Christ and the desire for everything that he loved and embraced, as Master Ignatius will point out at the conclusion of this fourth chapter (101–3).

Survey of the Text of Chapter 4 with Commentary

"Men Detached from the World and Determined to Serve God Totally"

The Society is composed of men who enjoy freedom as regards worldly values because they find their unity in their service of God.[2] They do not have to flee the world so much as to come out of themselves by laying aside the old man to be sent forth as a new man to live and proclaim the Gospel in this world. At the very beginning, Ignatius explains how the consequences of all this will entail concrete and firm decisions *in the area of poverty*. It is essential to renounce all possessions without any expectation of recovering them, even if this renunciation takes effect only by stages (53–59 and *NC* 32)

Next comes self-denial in one's relations with family and friends, including regular correspondence with them (60–62 and *NC* 53). One must accept an abnegation in the *whole area of affective relationships*. The Jesuit must become free internally not only with respect to his family but also with regard to certain friendships and to continued association with certain other groups.

Finally, there is the *renunciation of one's own self*; and this, of course, presupposes a genuine and warmhearted willingness to enter into the practice of fraternal correction within the Society (63 and *NC* 235–36). In particular, it presupposes the acceptance of criticisms that the superior could make after a fair assessment of the member's mistakes and defects. This is the path conducive to the formation of a community of charity and free exchange marked by simplicity, mutual respect, and service;

---

[2] The commentary on chapter 4 owes much to the study on the "Examen" published by Simon Decloux, S.J., in Constitutions of the Society of Jesus: *Incorporation of a Spirit*, ed. Dominique Bertrand, *CIS* (Rome: 1993), 134–43.

it will necessitate a genuine surrender of all self-seeking. Here we clearly see a characteristic of the vocation of the First Companions—a characteristic of which Fr. General has earnestly reminded us in the wake of GC 34.

The Experiences Characteristic of Our Vocation (64–79)

Having thus led the candidate into a kind of spiritual desert, Ignatius proceeds to introduce the major elements in the Jesuit novitiate that will determine his future, especially the six principal "experiments" or testing experiences. This plan was entirely unprecedented in his time, when novitiates were conducted entirely within the monastic confines. Nevertheless, Ignatius emphasized these experiences as essential elements in the early formation of candidates. The manner in which he speaks of them also shows more abundantly that we will find here some basic and permanent features that will mark the vocation of the Jesuit throughout his life. These experiences will develop the attitudes basic to the calling of the companion of Jesus to serve in a priestly body of apostles.

It may seem at first reading that these experiences are designed to be completed in a set sequence one after the other, but Ignatius actually allows for considerable flexibility (64, 71, CN 46). He accords superiors great freedom to consider circumstances of persons, time, place, culture, and the like, and to adapt accordingly. In proposing the experiences, Ignatius harks back to certain decisive moments in his own personal past and that of the First Companions as well. He knows from his own experience which are the aspects of a Jesuit life that he hopes to develop by means of each of these prescribed experiments. The candidate who asks to be admitted will need above all to understand and to share the spirit of the Society. The experiences will in turn help him to grasp that spirit and to live out certain specific, permanent elements of it.

These experiences are at one and the same time periods of testing and of formation. Each of them has a precise objective. Everything is based on one's experience of God (65: the Exercises made over a period of a month), followed by the self-effacement found in service out of love (66: the hospital); next comes the experience of poverty and reliance on God alone (67:

the pilgrimage), followed by the period of community service in the house (68) and, finally, by a life devoted to the apostolic ministry (69–70). These experiences provide a kind of practicum for the lesson of the Two Standards and initiate the novice into the personal, community, and apostolic demands of Jesuit life.

The *first experience* consists in making the Spiritual Exercises for one month (65). Ignatius explicitly demands a complete conversion and reconciliation with God, including the sacramental dimension. He then concentrates on the methods of prayer and on the contemplation of the gospel mysteries. Not everything about the Exercises is mentioned here—for example, nothing is said about the election, since the basic choice concerning the Society will normally have been made prior to entrance into the novitiate (51). Hence, the Exercises made for a month both during the novitiate and during the tertianship do not envision the choice of a state in life, even though this choice, already made, might well be confirmed during this period. Rather, the candidate strives for purity of conscience and learns to seek and find God in prayer and in life's experiences.

"The *second experience* is to serve for another month in hospitals or one of them" (66, emphasis added). Here the novice will share the life of the sick and the healthy alike, assisting and serving all. During this experience the novice cultivates a spirit of humility and self-effacement, demonstrating that he "completely gives up the world . . . so that in everything he may serve his Creator and Lord crucified for him" (66). The fundamental option of the Society includes, then, a complete availability for humble service in union with the passion of Christ handed over for the human race. This experience involves an opening to the apostolic life, since these are *the others* who call forth my generosity and my capacity for self-giving. This gift of one's self must not, however, be perfected through deeds of glory, but rather by imitating Christ, who became the servant of all. Such a preference for humble service, completely contrary to the search after personal honor and prestige, could not be authentically sustained over a long period unless supported by a contemplative impulse that suffuses this service with a genuine sense of communion with the Lord. Thus we come to appreciate how fully, in the mind of Ignatius, the apostolic purpose of the Society is rooted in and dependent upon contemplation.

"The *third experience* is to spend another month in making a pilgrimage" (67, emphasis added), dependent during this period on begging "for the love of Christ." The purpose here is twofold: first "to grow accustomed to discomfort in food and lodging"; and second, to train the candidate, "through abandoning all the reliance which he could have on money or other created things, [to] place . . . his reliance entirely in his Creator and Lord." The intention is to provide a genuine experience of poverty such as Ignatius and the early companions had undergone, something that had led them to a concrete experience of Providence as the intimate care of God for each individual. This feature of the life of the Society is closely bound up with availability and apostolic commitment.

"The *fourth experience* consists in the candidate's employing himself in the house . . . in various low and humble offices" (68, emphasis added) and "to do this with all diligence and care." Ignatius clearly wishes, as we see, to unite the companions in a simple, fraternal life wherein each one is ready to do his part in performing household tasks.

"The *fifth experience* is to explain the Christian doctrine to children or other simple persons" (69, emphasis added). However qualified they might be, all Jesuits belong to an apostolic body that seeks to serve the people of God, with a special preference for the poor. This is the best way not to forget the poor.

The *sixth experience* consists in preaching and hearing confessions (70, emphasis added). These final experiences highlight the apostolic and sacerdotal character of the body of the Society.

In light of these experiences, the candidate comes face to face with the Ignatian ideal: a humble apostle of the Lord, either a priest or a brother, dedicated to serve all those among whom he lives. To this end, he joins a community dedicated to mutual service. The Ignatian ideal envisions someone who has renounced "the world" in order to live in service to the Lord; by so doing, he discovers anew in prayer the mystery of Christ's compassionate love. He learns to rely entirely on the Lord as he offers himself to him to share in his mission. Presented with this ideal, the candidate is asked to make his own its interior summons and to give proof of his desire to respond and commit himself in faith and love. No. 71 adds that at least some of the experiences should be repeated prior to final vows, that is, during the third year of probation. The companion will then be able to embrace anew the deepest roots of his vocation to the Society of Jesus.

Ignatius also asks that each of the experiences be evaluated (73–79), and this again is undoubtedly part of the process by which superiors discern the authenticity of a given vocation. But looked at from a wider perspective, this points up the importance here of once more reflecting on each stage of development: "What growth has been observed and what are the difficulties that remain to be resolved?" This interest in evaluating activities and practices is closely linked to the habit of discernment.

Community Life in the House (80–90)

The rest of chapter 4 primarily concerns the life of the community within the house. Ignatius portrays here a peaceful house with a well-ordered sacramental life and a studious dedication to advancement in Christian doctrine (80). He then explains how it is necessary to exercise ourselves in poverty above all (81–82), humility, self-denial (82–83), and confidence in the Lord through obedience (84–90). These points will be treated in greater detail in Part III of the Constitutions. We simply note the spiritual dynamism that is at work in these paragraphs. As Ignatius sees it, the attitude of self-denial and the desire for spiritual progress developed by each individual will convince him that the poorest things in the house are actually best for him, and that thus all will best achieve equality and mutual fairness (81). Once again, the life of the First Companions is held up to us in the hope that we might "endeavor, as far as possible, to reach the same point as the earlier ones, or to go farther in the Lord" (81). No. 82 is animated by the same active gospel spirit. Even if it is not appropriate in this day and age to beg, certainly we are encouraged to dedicate some time and energy to ministries in the service of the poor and abandoned (*CN* 128, §5). The perspective enjoined here is explicitly theological, as evidenced by such phrases as "for the love of God our Lord," "in the service and for the glory of God"; so too is the insistence on availability for missions (82).

Humility will, however, be practiced in many more ways through service in the community, and Ignatius stipulates that "one should take on more promptly those tasks that offend his sensibilities more, if he has been ordered to do them" (83).

In the following paragraphs (84–89), Ignatius deals with training in obedience and emphasizes the essential connection between obedience and humility, using the example of the kitchen tasks (84). He communicates to the candidate the whole perspective of faith that is at the root of the fundamental practice of obedience in the Society. Obedience must above all be clearly understood in this light. It is a spiritual option freely chosen with God's grace. It cannot really be comprehended solely as if it had only a human aspect. Authority—no matter who is in command—is always exercised in the name of Christ. There is something quite abrupt in this manner of initially presenting obedience to the candidate. Here we observe an example of Ignatius's teaching style: at this stage, his technique is from the very start to move forthrightly to the heart of the matter, thus achieving greater clarity. When discussing the later stages of formation or the life of the Jesuit more fully formed, he will employ expressions that further clarify the matter.

Obviously, community life as such is not precisely and directly the subject of nos. 80–90. At the same time, it is also clear that the virtues being described will in fact facilitate a fraternal union firmly based on the Gospels (see *NC* 43, §2; 50, 51, and the index).

Manifestation of Conscience and Admission (91–100)

Beginning with no. 91, the style and tone of chapter 4 is notably elevated. This is the point at which Ignatius introduces the account of conscience. It involves a desire to live in a relationship of complete, sincere, and cordial openness with superiors. Thanks to this openness, the individuals will be better known in their interior life, so that thus the superior "may direct them . . . without placing them beyond the measure of their capacity in dangers or labors greater than they could in our Lord endure with a spirit of love," and so that the superior "may be better able to organize and arrange what is expedient for the whole body of the Society" (92). The manifestation of conscience is fundamental and quite unique to the Society. Ignatius explains how to practice this manifestation concretely (93–97) and suggests that it be "made in secret or in a manner more pleasing and consoling to [the candidate] with great humility, transparency, and charity" (93). This entire context shows that the account of conscience is not understood as an obligation binding under pain of sin, but rather as a grace freely received by a person conscious of a vocation to live his whole life in the Society (93–94).

In the course of these paragraphs on the account of conscience, Ignatius summarizes the process leading to final incorporation into the Society (98–100). Here is a clear sign that Ignatius regards the manifestation as essential to productive membership in the Society. We note also that admission is accompanied by reception of the sacraments of the Church, specifically by a general confession and by reception of Holy Communion.

Attachment to Christ Poor and Humble (101–103)

St. Ignatius concludes chapter 4 by recapitulating its message in a new way that clarifies, unifies, and gives effect to the spiritual path that he has proposed. He calls for the candidate to attach himself in his whole being to the person of *Christ poor and humble,* to Christ carrying the cross. This desire to identify with Jesus has its perfect expression in the Third Degree of Humility *(SpEx* 167), which in the Exercises is the attitude most essential for approaching a sound election. It is also a disposition of capital importance for one about to enter the Society. No. 101 of the Examen brings together the meditation on the Two Standards and the consideration of the Third Degree of Humility, "emphasizing . . . to how great a degree it helps and profits in the spiritual life to abhor in its totality and not in part whatever the world loves and embraces, and to accept and desire with all possible energy whatever Christ our Lord has loved and embraced." He is speaking here of Christ's way of life as revealed in the Gospels and the Beatitudes, going so far even as to accept "injuries, false accusations, and affronts, and to being held and esteemed as fools (but without their giving any occasion for this)." For the one who enters the Society, following Christ will consist in a genuine desire to put on the garment of Christ; this means that the sum of his desires must be centered on and unified around the person of Jesus, who is loved and faithfully followed as the One and Only.

This is the vision proposed. Now it will be necessary to begin learning how to live it. If the candidate, in his poverty of spirit, does not yet experience these desires, he might at least have the desire to experience them. If he answers in the affirmative, it is the sign of a man sufficiently open and disposed to accept the opportunities to grow and progress along this road, either within the house or outside it, that life might offer him. No. 102 introduces a note of Ignatian realism and practicality into the discussion, allowing it to descend from the world of aspirations and ideals to the realities of daily life.

PARTS I AND II: ADMISSION AND DISMISSAL

Part I: Admission to Probation

    Chap. 1: The Person Who Admits: Who?   PERSONS
                                          How?

    Chap. 2: The candidates: Who?
                                        Qualities?

    Chap. 3: Impediments to admission   CRITERIA
        excluding absolutely (164–76)
        rendering less apt (176–89)

    Chap. 4: Manner of dealing with those admitted   CIRCUMSTANCES
      1. Candidates-hosts: mutual information (190–196)
      2. First probation: reflection (197)
                  reading of the Examen and Formula (198–99)
                  manifestation of conscience (200)
      3. Second probation (end of 200) [=novitiate]
      4. Successive beginnings until the tertianship (202)

PART II: DISMISSAL

    Chap. 1. Those who can be dismissed (204–5)   PERSONS
                And the person deciding (206–8)

    Chap. 2: Causes for dismissal: If "one feels in our Lord" that
            to retain someone is   CRITERIA
        contrary to the glory of the Divine Majesty (210–211)
        contrary to what is best for the Society (212–15)
        contrary to what is best for the Society and the individual (216)
        contrary to what is best for external persons (217)

    Chap. 3: The Manner of Dismissing   CIRCUMSTANCES
    The manner that is most likely to give satisfaction in our Lord
        to the person dismissing:
          praying and requesting prayer (220)
          hearing the advice of others (221)
          putting aside bias and reflecting on the matter (222)
        to the one being dismissed:
          so that he leaves without shame and with all his belongings
            (223)
          with love and consolation in the Lord (225)
          with guidance toward God's service (226) →

Parts I and II · · · · · ·

ADMISSION TO PROBATION AND DISMISSAL OF THOSE WHO WERE ADMITTED BUT DID NOT PROVE THEMSELVES FIT

ORIGIN AND SOURCES OF PARTS I AND II

E ven before the official approbation of the Society, the companions were concerned about the admission of new members. Ignatius mentioned this in a letter of December 19, 1538, to Isabel Roser.[1] Beginning with the first version of the Formula of the Institute (*FI* 4 and especially 8), the subject regularly comes up. When Ignatius set to work on the *Constitutions* with Polanco as his secretary, the latter drafted a document dating from 1548 and entitled *Industriæ*.[2] Polanco himself stated that these *industriæ* recorded the thinking of Ignatius. Their organization is already very close to that of the future *Constitutions*. The second *industria* (that is, a practical means to a desired end) provides some criteria for the admission of candidates and some recommendations for making the right choice. This is the rough outline of what would become

---

[1] See Hugh Rahner, S.J., *Ignatius of Loyola: Letters to Women* (from the German original *Ignatius von Loyola: Briefwechsel mit Frauen*), trans. Kathleen Pond and S. A. H. Weetman (New York: Herder and Herder, 1960), 273.

[2] Juan de Polanco, S.J., in *Epistolæ et commentaria*, vol. 2 of *Polanci complementa*, vol. 54 of Monumenta historica Societatis Iesu (Madrid, 1917), 726–807.

Part I. In version *a* of 1550, the Examen was added at the end of this Part I as the fifth chapter. Later it was relocated to the beginning of the *Constitutions*.

As to Part II, dealing with dismissal, there is nothing in Polanco's *Industriæ* on this subject; it would seem that there was at first no thought of devoting a complete Part of the Constitutions to it. The constitutions of other religious orders do not speak of it as such, but limit themselves to a penal code, always associated with the idea of grave sanctions. Original even here, Ignatius did not desire a penal code. He wanted things to be done out of love, and did not want the Constitutions to oblige under pain of sin (602). He was, nevertheless, careful to specify not only the cases requiring dismissal but most especially the spirit in which the dismissal was to be carried out. This Part II, which we might fear would be the most severe and most juridical of all, turns out, surprisingly enough, to be the one most thoroughly marked by the charity and compassion of Ignatius.

PLACEMENT OF PARTS I AND II

The Examen (1–133) sets down the requirements for a vocation and provides a way of discerning whether or not the desire to enter actually comes from God. The Preamble (134–37) brings the candidate into a collaboration with God in the foundation of the Society. We are called upon to begin along with the One who continues to found the Society. As to Parts I and II (138–242), they invite us to enter into the human and divine interrelatedness that is the reality of every vocation. God continues to found the Society by calling men to join it.

Structure of Parts I and II

The outline on pages 37–38 indicates the analogous structure of the two parts. At first we are told of the *persons* who have the authority to admit or dismiss, and then of the *persons* to be admitted or dismissed. Next come the *criteria* or standards for admission or dismissal. Finally, the discussion turns to the *atmosphere* or spirit in which the decision is reached and the manner of dealing with the one admitted and the one asked to leave.

The contents of the various chapters in Parts I and II are, nevertheless, organized somewhat differently. This is clear from the outline just mentioned. We note especially that the *circumstances*, or manner of dismissal, discussed in Part II (chaps. 3 and 4) are considerably more detailed. Chapter 3 is, in fact, one of the most worked-over sections in the Constitutions, and it sets in clear relief the consideration and charity with which Ignatius wished this doleful procedure to unfold. Moreover, chapter 4 of Part II is at least unexpected. One would have imagined that the departure would be without hope of reversal. There is, to be sure, some element of sternness here, but it is accompanied by a concern for gentleness (236) and does not exclude the possibility that the companion might return. Chapter 4 ends on this positive note.

THE SUBJECT OF PARTS I AND II: VOCATIONS FOR THE GROUP

If one understands the Society and its Constitutions as a "pathway to God" (*FI* 1) that fleshes out the Spiritual Exercises by applying them to the whole of life, then Parts I and II correspond to Christ's call both in the Kingdom and in the Two Standards. Vocation comes at the outset in the plan of God, who calls for collaborators to praise and serve him there. Parts I and II help us go beyond the notion that vocation is a precise moment occurring in the past. Vocation always involves a choosing in the present, presupposing four separate agents: God who summons, the self who responds, the Church that accepts into its body, and the adversary. In this way, vocation is understood in its divine as well as human dimensions as a present and permanent beginning, a yes that perdures on my part and on the part of the Society as well.

Right now God is calling each one of us just as we are, inviting us to be part of the Society just as it is. During the tertianship we are urged to reread Parts I and II, seeing them as relevant to our lives in the present, while we are about to assume our proper share of responsibility for the group.

The possibility of dismissal and departure also needs to be considered. It is always possible for me to leave or to be dismissed. Therefore, it is not accurate to say that this has no relevance for me. Think of St. Francis of Assisi, who mentioned to Brother Leo that he felt himself capable of abandoning everything, or of the ancient father who prayed every day for perseverance. Sometimes we would like to have perfect security, complete human assurance. But perseverance is a grace, a pure gift of God to be received with humble gratitude. It is true, of course, that someone can get to the point of remaining in the group while actually being outside it, not being fully identified with it. It is not healthy to have reasons only for staying. There are always the yes and no, the for and against staying. What gives effective force to my yes is the free choice I make today to give my whole being to God, who is the source of everything.

For every religious order, the question of vocations is one of life or death. Out of the ten parts of his Constitutions, St. Ignatius dedicates two to the matter of vocations. Indeed, one might even say three or four parts, since the Examen and Part III both treat of this as well. In his preparatory documents, in the first *industria* in particular, Polanco proposes a complete pastoral approach to vocations, along with eighteen concrete suggestions. These include prayers for vocations, being where there are young people, frequent conversations, giving the Exercises, maintaining a presence at universities and in important cities. But Ignatius did not retain this *industria*, which had originally been placed within Part I of text *A* (1550). With the passage of time, he became more demanding with respect to admissions, insisting that the desire to admit new candidates be tempered (143). One has only to compare no. 144 as it appears in text *A* with its counterpart in text *B* (dating from 1556). True, in Ignatius's day there were vocations in abundance. But what about today, especially in the Northern Hemisphere? Do we have a genuine concern for vocations to the Society? What is our attitude toward this question? We might do well to heed the congress held in July 1997 at Loyola, followed by the letter of Fr. General to the whole Society in September 1997.

CERTAIN SPIRITUAL HIGHLIGHTS OF PARTS I AND II

Here are some keys that might contribute to a Spirit-assisted reading of these parts of the Constitutions.

Theological Insight

The primary purpose of Parts I and II is to furnish criteria by which vocations to the Society might be discerned. Such criteria might have appeared as chiefly utilitarian, but in point of fact the criteria found in these two parts are rooted in deep theological considerations. Certain recurring expressions maintain this strong theological emphasis: "the service of God our Lord" (thirty-six times), "in our Lord" (twenty-two times), "for the glory and praise of God our Lord" (fourteen times). This recalls the beginning of the *Spiritual Exercises:* "Man is created to praise, reverence, and serve God our Lord" (*SpEx* 23). What the Exercises propose as the final purpose of all human beings becomes in the Constitutions the specific purpose of the Society itself. Divine service, zeal for souls, and a desire to help them achieve their final purpose (see 156)—those are the fundamental signs pointing toward a possible vocation to the Society.

But God is not just the final purpose of the Society and of every Jesuit; he is also the beginning and the origin. Vocation is a pure gift of God, and all the natural and infused gifts flow from him. This least Society of Jesus is an instrument of which God avails himself (190). His initiative brought it into being (134 and 812), and everything begins and ends in him.

We underline again that the election according to the third time, always present here, is made "in our Lord" in the context of prayer (229). Admission or dismissal—everything is done in the sight of God, in pursuit of his will, in order "to cooperate with the divine motion and vocation" (144). The superior is asked to consider and to ponder in the Lord, to feel in the Lord, and to understand better in the Lord. Thus will he judge what seems "more suitable in the Lord for his divine service in the Society" (143).

The Permanent Presence of the Apostolic Objective

The service of God and the welfare of souls are like a refrain throughout Part I, appearing as the foremost criterion for the discernment of vocations to the Society, overshadowing all the others in chapters 2 and 3. This is quite specific for Ignatius, in contrast, for example, with the rule of St. Benedict, where the fundamental criterion is "Does he really seek God?" If some doubt might have persisted with regard to the coadjutor brothers, the Complementary Norms completely removed it (CN 81, 83, 98, 243). Concerning the question of dismissal in Part II, the basic criterion is the injury done to the social body of the Society (189, 212, 222), since the apostolic purpose is achieved in and through the entire group. Clearly evident, however, is the context of charity full of discernment and sensitivity with which Master Ignatius wanted dismissals to be carried out.

Atmosphere of Discernment and Election in the Third Time

When beginning to read Parts I and II, we must not concentrate right away on the juridical norms that are necessary in all their rigor, yet are always laid down in terms of the fundamental criterion, the apostolic goal. What is more original with Ignatius is the arrangement of these essential considerations. Everything is organized so as to facilitate an election in the third time (*SpEx* 177–83). It is recommended to confide the question to the Lord in prayer (193), to consult with others (194–96), to weigh reasons for and against (147, 189), and to allow oneself to be instructed by the divine Wisdom (161). The work of Ignatius on the *Constitutions* can be summed up as an invitation to make an election. The admission of a candidate is clearly the result of this spiritual discernment and an election. This attitude of spiritual discernment allows us to make good use of objective criteria and to evaluate them in the light of the fundamental one, which is always the welfare and the salvation of souls for the greater glory of God. A reading of declarations 162, 176, 178, and 186 will confirm this. We note again that in chapter 4 of Part I the first probation, immediately before entering the novitiate, is conducted in this spirit, and the steps are prescribed in some detail (197–200). Clearly, Ignatius wanted the entrance into the novitiate to be, to the greatest extent possible, like an election and a definitive determination to enter the Society and "to live and die therein" (191, 194).

When a dismissal is being considered, this process of discernment is emphasized even more. There are few passages in the Constitutions where the stages in the process of discernment and decision are so precisely set down as in chapter 3 of Part II (220–222). Here the context, the spirit, of the Exercises is clearly presupposed, specifically the Principle and Foundation (*SpEx* 23), the Third Class of Men (*SpEx* 155), and the election in the third time.

One recalls that in the General Examen, which takes place at the time of admission (146, 198), the dialogue proceeds after the manner of an election of the *second* time (*SpEx* 177). The candidate is expected to accept willingly what is being proposed, to be happy with it, and to feel that it fulfills his deepest desire. For the Society, on the other hand, and for its representative, the superior, the discernment and the election unfold more after the manner of the *third* time. The superior is expected to weigh before God the reasons for and against. The whole process of admission as just described is marked by this great concern for forthright honesty and clarity.

The Importance of Charity at the Time of Dismissal or Departure

In his introduction to Part II, Fr. Diaz Moreno has written enlightening pages on this subject of charity toward one who is leaving the Society.[3] He points out that a calm and perceptive reading of Part II can often result in a real surprise. This Part of the Constitutions is, after all, devoted to the difficult and thorny topic of dismissal. One might reasonably fear that it would be dominated by a cold legalism, in contrast with other sections characterized by a lofty theological and spiritual outlook. Nevertheless, even though the necessary juridical elements are present, still one's attention is drawn more to the deep spiritual quality suffusing the text. Perhaps the heart of Ignatius is revealed here more openly than elsewhere in the

---

[3] See Diaz Moreno, in Arzubialde, *Constituciones*, 119–20.

Constitutions. It is the heart of a father who knows how to balance the common good of the Church and the Society with the particular good of an individual. The better service of God remains, of course, the guiding principle behind every disposition involving departures as well as dismissals. The expression "divine service" recurs some twenty times. It always guided Ignatius, but here it exhibits a powerful aura of companionship in Christ. From the outset of this Part II, one can perceive a typically Ignatian conviction that it should be more difficult to dismiss than to admit (204), evidence of his respect and affection for the members of the Society, to whom he felt himself so closely bound as companions of Jesus. A departure or dismissal, at whatever stage it might occur, always affects the entire group. The stronger the bonds of gratitude, the more difficult it will be to dismiss (205). This explains to some extent the extraordinary patience Ignatius displayed toward certain truly worthy companions who were, nonetheless, in flagrant conflict with the government of the order. One thinks of Bobadilla and especially Rodrigues.[4]

At the beginning of chapter 2, where the causes for dismissal are spelled out with considerable strictness, Ignatius added declaration 211, revealing his opposition to all narrow legalism. He relied on "the discreet zeal of those who have charge of the matter" to reach the final decision. "The more difficulty and doubt they have, the more will they commend the matter to God our Lord and the more will they discuss it with others who can be helpful toward perceiving the divine will in the matter" (211). Such is the Christlike heart of Ignatius, who dwells four more times in this same chapter on the charity to be practiced when dealing with cases of dismissal (209, 213, 214, 217).

In the same way, chapter 3 witnesses to the pastoral sensitivity with which Ignatius wanted the invariably saddening process of dismissal to be carried out. The goal would be to send the party away with as much love in his heart for the house and as much consolation in our Lord as possible (225; also see 226 and 229). Finally, in the extraordinary fourth

---

[4] See letters 3417, 3547, 3584, 3605, 4206, 5329, and 5799 in any collection of Ignatius's letters.

chapter, when he mentions the possibility of readmission, Ignatius suggests that one act with "a spirit of gentleness, taking into account the good of the subject won back and the edification of those in the house," while leaving the decision to the discretion of the one with authority. On this hopeful note Part II comes to a close.

PART III: THE PRESERVATION AND PROGRESS OF THOSE IN PROBATION

Chap. 1: The preservation pertaining to the soul and to progress in virtue

Introduction (243): Presentation of the plan of Part III

    1. Progress in Spirit (244–76)

        a. An atmosphere for "progress in spirit" (244–52): separation (244–49); change of "conversation," guarding the senses, silence and discretion in speech, the image of God in others (250), manner of taking meals (251)

        b. Spiritual progress made through practice and spiritual exercises: occupation (253), poverty (254–59), discernment of spirits (260), examen of conscience and the sacraments (261)

        c. Aids to awaken the spirit: fidelity (263) and humility (265), discreet penance (269), and correction (270), a syndic (271), illness (272), unity (273)

    2. Progress in virtue (276–79)

        Progress in spirit rooted in "stable" habits (virtue). Example of the ancients (276), study of doctrine, training in the spiritual life (277), preaching (280), exercises of humility and charity (282), the vows of devotion (283), obedience (284–86), poverty (287), purity of intention and seeking God in all things (288), practices of humility and virtue (289–91)

Chap. 2: Preservation of the body (292–306)

Spirit incarnated in the body, all integrated, "stabilized"

    1. The physical body (292–302)

        taking care of one's body (292)

        daily order, repose, sleeping, rising, (294), food, clothing, (295) work, (298) penance (300)

    2. The social body (303–6):

        the prefect of health (303), the sick (304), those in charge of offices (305), launderer, barber (306)

Part III · · · · · ·

THE PRESERVATION AND PROGRESS OF THOSE WHO REMAIN IN PROBATION

PLACEMENT AND TOPIC OF PART III

The introductory paragraph (243) clearly explains the place of Part III in the general plan of the Constitutions. The person called and admitted (Parts I and II) becomes a disciple (Parts III and also IV). True to the developmental dynamism of the Constitutions, Part III will introduce the very first stage in formation. And the purpose of this first stage is to foster the young Jesuit's "progress both in spirit and in virtues . . . in such a manner as care is also taken of [his] health and bodily strength." Part III, which deals with life within the "houses," is closely linked to Part IV, which will treat Jesuit students living in the "colleges." For Ignatius these two steps in the formation process really form a whole (243, 135, 137), since the studies must always be rooted in, based upon (see 307, 814), progress in the spiritual life and in the virtues that emanate from it.

Although Part III concentrates on a precise period in the life of a Jesuit, it also sets in relief certain abiding characteristics of a companion of Jesus. Just as a Jesuit's vocation is a reality always present to him, so is formation a continuing and ongoing necessity. Numerous passages from Part III can be found in the small book called *Our Jesuit Life* (formerly known as the *Summary of the Constitutions*); these treat of matters that concern us all.[1] Part III claims, therefore, a prominent place in the organic perspective of the Constitutions. It is devoted to the initial formation of the Jesuit admitted to the novitiate, but it also presents a spiritual pedagogy calculated to prepare the way for what will be proposed in those subsequent parts dealing with the Jesuit who is fully formed and on mission. Consequently, in Part III we learn how to cultivate those spiritual qualities necessary for the life of fully formed companions of Jesus (Part VI), for the accomplishment of the apostolic mission (Part VII), for the necessary union of the entire group (Part VIII), and for the best possible preparation of the kind of individual portrayed in the description of the superior general (Part IX). In addition, Part X is a sort of subdivision of Part III: as their respective titles indicate, both parts list means aimed at preservation, growth, and advancement, whether it be for the entire group (Part X) or for the young Jesuit (Part III). We are justified, therefore, in claiming for Part III a key role in the development of the Constitutions. Despite its very simple appearances, it affords spiritual instructions and insights whose efficacy in the various forms of life in the Society will reveal itself in the parts to follow.

PURPOSE OF FORMATION

As stated in the first paragraph (243), the purpose of formation is to enable the young recruits "to make progress along the path of the divine service," in order that "they might work in the vineyard of the Lord." This apostolic direction and purpose will be repeated throughout Part III (273, 291, 292) and, indeed, throughout the Constitutions, particularly in the opening paragraph of each Part. For Ignatius, all of formation—spiritual, intellectual, and cultural—was directed toward the apostolate. Ignatius certainly opted for an integration of culture, but always with the unwavering concern that formation be oriented entirely toward the service of God and the spiritual welfare of others. He knew from experience how the temptation to backslide could surface during the long years of preparation. The

---

[1] *Our Jesuit Life* (St. Louis: Institute of Jesuit Sources, 1990).

risk of regarding one's progress as a means of self-promotion or personal advancement could never be casually discounted. The education and formation of the young Jesuit would certainly permit the development of the gifts that God had bestowed on him, yet the primary purpose is to enhance his effectiveness as a member of an apostolic body in the service of its mission. As part of the training, the candidate will acquire culture, but at the same time the apostolic enterprise must not be turned to one's own personal profit or rendered purely secular. Throughout its history right up to the present day, this has been a tremendous challenge for the Society. We will see in Part IV what devices Ignatius employed to meet that challenge.

HISTORY OF PART III

Both Parts III and IV are the fruit of a long process. From the very foundation of the Society, Ignatius began to work on the question of formation. Already in the Formula of the Institute of 1540, there is mention of a long formation (*FI* 9) and also of "colleges"; however, the latter were understood as houses in which students lived but did not attend classes. Ignatius devoted greater exertions to the composition and editing of these two parts than he did to any other Part of the Constitutions. He did not finally complete Part III until shortly before his death. As to Part IV, it was the only Part left unfinished at the time of his death. It was necessary to conform to the complex canonical and religious legislation of the time, as well as to the kind of religious formation that was customary then. In fact, the prevailing system was actually quite austere, involving strict controls, rigid discipline, and blind submission. Under the inspiration and insight of his own Spiritual Exercises, Ignatius simply developed another more humane and more spiritual pedagogy favoring an education for freedom that depended on personal responsibility and mutual support. Something of a pioneer in his time, he also acknowledged that to some extent he had to incorporate the methods common at this time. Often these labored under the weight of their years, though they also reflected the fruits of rich experience. Consequently, Part III embodies precious elements borrowed from the wisdom of the older religious orders. To gather such gems, Polanco will pore over the most influential rules of the past—Benedictine, Dominican, and Franciscan. Part IV of the eventual Constitutions incorporates the educational system of the time, specifically the "Modus Parisiensis," that is, the educational system followed at the university of Paris, a system quite different from what Ignatius had experienced in Spain. But along with these invaluable contributions, the two parts inevitably contain certain detailed prescriptions tied to the contemporary culture. Among these are the radical separation from outsiders (244), censorship of correspondence (246), the assigned confessor (261), exclusion of women (266), the prohibition of musical instruments and weapons (266–68). Today the cultural milieu has changed. Human relations have become less formal and more spontaneous. We pay more attention to the integration of affectivity and to the gospel freedom in our relationships. On this level, the recent general congregations have decreed certain necessary updatings, which are compiled in the Complementary Norms (*CN* 44–56).

Freed by the Complementary Norms from these particular prescriptions reflecting an earlier period, we are now ready to immerse ourselves in a spiritually enlightened reading of Part III, so that we can sense its underlying dynamic and the inspiration pervading it. But the essence of its originality consists in the arrangement of the whole, so organized as to enhance a progressive development of personal responsibility rather than to foster the external observance of disciplinary regulations. It is a matter of learning to live in a habitual state of discernment and election. Some of the guideposts, often mirroring the wisdom of the older orders, are arranged so that the young Jesuits might prepare themselves "to progress on their own in the spiritual life and in virtue" (137). This text voices the hope that by the end of the novitiate the young religious will have learned how to progress on his own. This original arrangement of the material is what enables Part III to maintain its perennial relevance.

THE CONNECTION BETWEEN PART III AND CHAPTER 4 OF THE EXAMEN

To read Part III correctly, we must not fail to note its connection with chapter 4 of the Examen. There, as we have seen, Ignatius presented features specific to the Society, among them the spiritual and apostolic attitudes that candidates are urged to begin cultivating during the novitiate, in particular through the "experiences." This chapter 4 furnishes the key to a correct interpretation of Part III, which, without reference to the Examen, would only lead to a monastic type of novitiate oblivious to the apostolic and missionary dimension of formation. It is equally true, however, that chapter 4 without Part III would lack the realism needed to integrate a progressive formation amid the ordinary occurrences of daily life in community. The novice requires a spiritual formation nourished by the wisdom of the ancients (Part III), but he must also prepare, perhaps with even greater care, to be sent on mission, plunged into the affairs of the world (*GenEx* 4). It would be reasonable to say that chapter 4 of the Examen begins to implement the fundamental *attitudes* and insights of the Exercises (the Kingdom, the Standards, the Third Degree of Humility) by calling for them to be put into practice amid the situations and restrictions encountered during the *experiences*, whereas Part III implements the spiritual *educational method* of the Exercises in the course of a regular daily routine.

EXPLANATION OF THE STRUCTURAL PLAN OF PART III

The Difference between the Plan of Text *a* and That of Text *B*

Anyone glancing at the outline printed on p. 46 would at first sight regard Part III, taken as a whole, as little more than a loosely organized collection of wise counsels and spiritual directives. There is, however, an original structure here, and it reveals an existential dynamic that Master Ignatius employs in his development of the Constitutions. Fr. Dominique Bertrand demonstrates this in chapter 3 of his book *Un Corps pour l'Esprit*, mentioned earlier. It will be helpful to understand this if we first recall the history of the text. A comparison of Part III in the text of 1550 (text *a*) with that in our present text of 1556 (text *B*; see the table found in the introductory chapter, p. 10 above) shows that the order of the two chapters was reversed in these two editions. The earlier version begins with a first chapter on the preservation of the body and then in the following chapter deals with the preservation of the soul and with progress in virtue. Text *B*, on the other hand, begins with the chapter on the preservation of the soul and advancement in virtues and then goes on in chapter 2 to treat the preservation of the body. By inverting the chapters, Ignatius reveals a characteristic perspective of his spiritual pedagogy: for him, progress in the spiritual life consists in being incarnated more and more in the group. Rather than propose a dynamic of spiritualization that runs the risk of disincarnation, he introduces the novice into a personal incarnational process and an encounter with the real. To be sure, he hopes with all his heart that the novice will be moved by noble desires. That is fundamental and was, in fact, the genesis of his own conversion (*PilgTest* nos. 9–20). He looks for this from the beginning of the Exercises (annotation 5) and throughout chapter 4 of the Examen. Nevertheless, once these desires have been awakened, they should not become mere dreams or lead to illusion (he well remembered his own experience during the early days in Manresa), but should be firmly rooted in reality. It is this path of incarnation in reality, of descent and profound immersion into the human condition, that Ignatius proposes in the pedagogy of Part III. By reversing the order of the two chapters, Ignatius left a clear sign. As Fr. Dominique Bertrand writes, "To conclude Part III with a chapter on the preservation of the body simply makes a statement that the only genuine spiritual life is a realistic one."[2]

The Plan of Part III

The candidate arrives at the novitiate with great desires in the Lord. Ignatius clearly welcomes these desires and this enthusiasm. Bent on helping the novice to progress spiritually,

---

[2] *Un Corps*, 102.

Ignatius will propose certain means that will allow him to fully welcome these gifts from God, to foster and strengthen them. In chapter 1, he begins by establishing a milieu (244–52) designed to promote awareness and progress in spirit in the novice, who is expected to train himself through a number of spiritual practices (253–62) and to be aided in various ways (263–75). This arousal of the spirit is gradually to sink root into a way of being and living that gains stability and firmness in the evangelical virtues that Master Ignatius considered essential to the apostolate of a companion of Jesus (276–91). In chapter 2, the incarnational process advances through a concern for integrating and appropriately mastering one's own body. As is evident in no. 292, this activity already presupposes a certain ability to practice spiritual discernment that one hopes the efforts described in chapter 1 have fostered in him. In this way, the novice comes to perceive on his own what is suitable for him according to the Lord in the different areas of his life and his personal (293–302) and social (303–6) surroundings. We cannot fail to note, of course, that Part III concludes somewhat prosaically with a comment on the launderer and the barber. Here again we encounter an example of the Ignatian spiritual realism ever mindful of the concrete and the practical.[3]

SOME MAJOR MILEPOSTS IN PART III

An Original Dynamic of Life in the Spirit

After thus rapidly scanning the plan of Part III as rearranged by Ignatius in text *B*, we perceive the original dynamic of life in the Spirit that he devised.[4] In the earlier text *a*, which is less dynamic than its later version, the spiritual life is represented as an ascent toward the Spirit and toward a gradual spiritualization. In text *B*, Ignatius sees it as more a matter of descent. The spirit is allowed to immerse itself in the concrete

---

[3] Also see no. 827, the last paragraph in the Constitutions, which emphasizes the importance of healthful air!

[4] Simon Decloux provides a more detailed analysis of the material in this section in his essay entitled "Examen," in Bertrand, *Incorporation of a Spirit*, 163–95.

details of daily life by means of spiritual and corporal exercises undertaken during the experiences and in community within the house, until the body and the new life in the Spirit come to be integrated. Perceptible here is an allusion to the descent of Christ, who took the path of the poor and humble servant, a path to which the novice asks to be admitted during the Second Week of the Exercises as he prays the colloquy of the Two Standards (*SpEx* 146, 147). Here too, on the one hand, a dynamic of incarnation gets under way, allowing everyone to accept himself progressively in his personal reality, his gifts, and his limitations. On the other hand, a dynamic of incorporation into the social body of the Society also begins. This twofold dynamic of integration will continue and work itself out fully in the parts of the Constitutions to follow.

A Basic Theological Perspective

Paying too much attention to the disciplinary and ascetical practices proposed in Part III risks the serious mistake of measuring the spiritual life by the observance of rules and regulations. But for Ignatius the spiritual life was, above all, a dialogue of exchange. In this dialogue God is always the first to offer and give himself, as we see in the development of the *Spiritual Exercises* and their culmination in the Contemplation to Obtain Love. The human person can accomplish nothing that God has not given him to do. Ignatius will always keep this theological perspective in the forefront, as is clear in certain paragraphs of Part III:

▸ No. 250 opens a theological and contemplative path toward the heart of fraternal relations.

▸ No. 282 introduces the novice to a mutual exchange with God through a humble and loving participation in fraternal life. See also the inspiring no. 283.

▸ No. 288, which is sometimes called the jewel of Part III, leads into a spiritual life centered on the gratuity of God's gift received and returned through continual purity of intention and the search for God in all things.

These attitudes are not mere details of a life in the Spirit. Rather they completely encompass it and lead the person to

God's plan of salvation and to participation in the love of the Trinity at work in the world.

But once again Ignatius is always the realist. In the developmental structure of the Constitutions, he is careful not to stint on the stages of the spiritual pedagogy leading to that life in the Spirit, lest it remain a misty dream. Hence the need to recognize the resistance and the obstacles that remain, and to summon us to conversion and a purification of the heart [to be achieved] through ascetical exercises and practices and through the acquisition of true and solid virtues (260), including even the integration of the body itself. This is the path that he developed in Part III, where the perspective is entirely centered on God, theological, and attentive to realistic practices.

Pedagogy Influenced by the Teaching Methods of the Spiritual Exercises

At this stage of the formation process, all the directives are suffused by the pedagogy of the Spiritual Exercises; for example,

- the importance of solitude and favorable circumstances at the outset of the spiritual life (244–49, 276)

- the necessity of instruction and the discussion that accompanies it (263, 244, 276)

- the integration of the body (292), all the faculties, and the senses into the life of the spirit (250)

- practice in living a true sacramental life (277), along with examination of one's life and the discernment of spirits (260), which will gradually lead the novice to take responsible charge of his own life (292)

- the emphasis on humility and charity (282), which leads directly to the contemplation of Christ, the poor and humble servant totally delivered over to humankind and giving the ultimate demonstration of love

- the practice of the Spiritual Exercises (277, 279), which will set the novice to living more and more the Contemplation for Obtaining Love, learning to make his whole life a loving dialogue with God (288)

This pedagogy of the Spiritual Exercises also reveals itself in the attitudes of those in charge of formation: discretion and discernment, which stimulates and trains a person to take charge of himself in the Lord; development by means of concrete exercises and practices that aid them to test personal dispositions realistically and to acquire necessary habits (280–281); awareness also of the weakness of the human condition despite goodwill (269–73). In particular, see no. 270 and note the emphasis placed on love there, all the more so when it is necessary to admonish someone.

The Role of the Master of Novices (263)

Ignatius stresses the confidential relationship that should prevail between this faithful and competent man and the novices in his charge. This is a necessary condition if they are to be able to open themselves to him without reserve in all that pertains to their lives, including their weaknesses as well as their successes. From experience Master Ignatius knew how deeply one's spiritual progress and fidelity to God help to advance a privileged relationship with another who has witnessed his exertions and struggles and the graces he has received. Because the Spiritual Exercises are themselves a profoundly personal experience, we are not surprised that Ignatius would pay such attention to the personal nature of the spiritual life, and assign so decisive a role to the personal spiritual guide of young Jesuits in formation. In the not too distant past, one could see great value in fidelity to rules and structures. Without at all discounting their legitimate place, we have more recently emphasized the relationship between each individual and his guide, or a total relationship of trust. This personalized, regular, and open spiritual direction is now accepted as basic and essential to the entire formation experience.

Formation for the Evangelical Virtues of the Vows

This formation is not developed as such in Part III. But the theological perspective is there, along with the pedagogy of the Exercises and the concrete and demanding attitudes that they summon up. These create an atmosphere from which, one can hope, such a formation will emerge automatically. It is true, however, that in these secularized times, often so hostile to certain gospel values, the evangelical virtues of the vows demand a more explicit reflection, as do the clear spiritual options available to the young throughout their lives. GCs 31, 32, and 33, the guidance afforded by the Complementary Norms, and the directives of both Fr. General and the Church at large clarify and update the broad and simple provisions of the Constitutions. One should note, however, that in this Part III Ignatius, true to the developmental progression of the Constitutions, does make quite clear how poverty (254–59, 285, 287) and obedience (284–86) are to be observed during this first stage in formation. He stresses the asceticism necessary for someone who is striving to interiorize an attitude of obedience. Later he will not address himself in quite the same way to scholastics (Part IV), to the fully formed Jesuit (Part VI), or to the Jesuit on mission (Part VII). As regards poverty, Ignatius expects an interior attitude to form during the course of the novitiate itself. As this stage begins (254, 257), he sets the novice to performing specific acts by which he exercises poverty. The hope is that later, after the virtue has matured, the young religious will discover poverty "as a mother" (287) who unceasingly brings us forth into a life of complete confidence in God alone.

PART IV: THE LEARNING AND OTHER MEANS OF HELPING THEIR NEIGHBOR THAT ARE TO BE IMPARTED TO THOSE WHO ARE RETAINED IN THE SOCIETY

Preamble: The need for the colleges (307–8)
Chaps. 1 and 2: Institution of the colleges
1. The founders and benefactors (309–19)
2. Acceptance of the foundation (320–325)
3. Property, administration, and income (326–32)
Chaps. 3 to 9: the scholastics
1. Requisite qualities (chap. 3. [333–38])
2. Care of health and spiritual life (chap. 4. [339–50])
   N.B. time and manner of prayer (340–341; 342–45)
3. Intellectual formation (chaps. 5 to 7 [351–91])
   what to study (chap. 5. [351–59]): subject matter, curriculum, doctrine
   how to study (chap. 6. [360–391])
   purity of intention (360–362); teaching methods (374–90)
   classes in the colleges (chap. 7) [added in part after the death of Ignatius]
4. Apostolic life (chap. 8 [400–414])
   necessary by reason of the Society's purpose (400, cf. 351, 446)
   primary characteristic: practical character
   celebration of Mass; preaching; sacraments; the Eucharist, confession; giving the Exercises, catechizing children and the unlettered
   aid to the dying
   Epilogue: spiritual conversation, unction of the Holy Spirit, disposition to receive divine grace
5. Interruption of studies (chap. 9)
Chap. 10: government of the colleges
1. Who has authority?
2. The rector: qualities (423), office (424–27)
3. Aids to good government (428–36)
4. Spiritual ministries of the college
Chaps. 11 to 17: The Society's universities
1. Acceptance of universities and the reasons for this (440, Chap. 11)
2. Subjects that should be taught; faculties of theology and arts; medicine and law not undertaken (chap. 12: 452)
   Educational norms (chaps. 12 to 15): teaching methods (chap. 13), manuals (chap. 14), courses and degrees (chap. 15)
3. Religious and moral education (chap. 16)
4. Governance (chap. 17)

Part IV · · · · · ·

THE LEARNING AND OTHER MEANS OF HELPING THEIR NEIGHBOR THAT ARE TO BE IMPARTED TO THOSE WHO ARE RETAINED IN THE SOCIETY

THE THEME OF PART IV AND ITS COMPLEXITY

The subject of Part IV is stated in its title as well as in its prologue (307–8). Now that the subject of spiritual formation has been developed in the previous Part, Part IV expands upon the intellectual and pastoral training of those who enter the Society of Jesus. From the outset it aligns itself with the developmental dynamic of the Constitutions in its intimate connection with Part III (see 243 and 307). No. 308 explains how this stage of formation came into existence. It would be fair enough to call it "the history of a disappointment."[1] St. Ignatius and his early companions had hoped to admit young candidates who, like themselves, had already completed their studies. Rapidly disillusioned on this score, they soon received young men who had not yet made their studies and would, after completing their novitiate, require all the intellectual and pastoral formation that would allow them to develop and properly prepare themselves for the priestly ministry. The term "college" designated the house in which these young recruits lived in community while attending classes in the local university, just as the First Companions did at the

---

[1] D. Bertrand, "Un mariage avec la culture," Christus Collection, no. 117 (Jan. 1983), 105–8.

university of Paris. At first, therefore, the college was simply a residence for young Jesuits in studies and not a school offering courses. But as we continue to read Part IV, we will note that with the passage of time the college became a place where classes were held, and that even later the same would be true of the Society's universities. Furthermore, these institutions provided formation not only for the Jesuit scholastics but also for extern students (see chaps. 11–17). Hence the complexity of Part IV, whose original theme looked to the education of only Jesuits but eventually expanded to include many others.

The Plan, History, and Meaning of Part IV

Glancing over Part IV as a whole and at the outline on page 60, we note that this is the longest Part of the Constitutions, containing 203 articles out of the entire 827, or a fourth of the whole work. It is the only Part to begin with a preamble (307–8), and it is the only Part left incomplete at the death of Ignatius. Chapters 12 to 17 seem at first to be repetitions of chapters 3 to 10. All of this suggests a long history and indicates that Part IV was put together gradually and in stages; thus, one might say, it mirrors the progressive development of the nascent Society as it became involved in the culture of the times and in its own educational commitments. In its earliest version, represented in texts *a* and *A* (1550), the content was limited to chapters 1–6 and 8–10 of the present work. In this first phase, it envisioned only the training of Jesuit scholastics, allowing for certain exceptions (see 338). Similarly, the colleges were merely places of residence where these scholastics lived and attended to their spiritual, intellectual, and pastoral formation. Text *B* (1556) has chapter 7 in addition, dealing with extern students. This shows, of course, that these externs were already being admitted to the classes and to the colleges by the end of Ignatius's life. As to the section pertaining to the universities (chaps. 11–17), this had been drawn up by Ignatius in 1554 as separate constitutions for the universities that the Society was beginning to administer.

Ignatius had left two blank pages in the text *B* version of Part IV. He intended to use them in a revised version of the articles concerning the universities, the essence of which would be inserted into the Constitutions. But he died before he could bring this project to completion. Probably in an effort to implement his wishes, those carrying on his work transferred the bulk of these special constitutions into text *B*. That accounts for the length of these chapters and for some repetition of material already covered in chapters 1–10. It also explains the asymmetry of Part IV when compared to the Constitutions as a whole.

The presence of this long series of chapters in Part IV proves interesting. The very texts themselves show how gradually Ignatius and the companions came to accept responsibility for the educational needs first of the colleges and then of the universities. Thus they entered actively into the world of culture, contrary to what they had intended in the beginning. Concern for the formation of the scholastics expands in Part IV to an apostolic preoccupation that, though perfectly appropriate for the Society, might seem more relevant to Part VII. From the very outset, there existed, we can see, a direct link between the training of the young companions and the work of educating others. Again we note an example of the strong apostolic dynamism of the First Companions. Once opened to externs, the colleges rapidly grew into a separate apostolate quite distinct from the direct training of Jesuit scholastics. This movement prefigures and even justifies, insofar as it is necessary, an evolution taking place in recent years. Many scholasticates of the Society have recently admitted extern students to pursue the same courses as the Jesuits. Is that not something of an unexpected return to our origins, entailing an apostolic responsibility of the Society towards the non-Jesuit students in these colleges and universities?

SOME MAJOR THEMES OF PART IV

Part IV reflects the era of Ignatius in its concrete provisions more than does any other Part of the Constitutions. As we go through this Part, it is important to pay attention to the footnotes that indicate how to implement and update the texts, with frequent reference to the Complementary Norms. Even so, these texts from the Constitutions still emit a certain spirit that even today retains its vigor and its ability to affect us, and still yields criteria relevant to the objectives and activities of the universities of the Society as a whole and of their various departments. Rather than furnish a detailed analysis, in the following pages we will simply highlight certain major themes that display the power of these objectives and criteria even today.[2]

Spiritual Formation: Chapter 4

No. 340 contains the two complementary principles that aim at unifying the life of studies and the spiritual life of Jesuit scholastics. They are counseled that, on the one hand, "[c]are must be taken that they do not through fervor in study grow cool in their love of true virtues and of religious life" and, on the other hand, that "they will not have much place for mortifications or for long prayers and meditations." This balance sought and laid out by Ignatius grows out of "a pure intention in the service of God." It is the same God who is to be praised and served by both prayer and study.

The paragraphs that follow deal with the form of private prayer and the time to be spent in it. Concerning the *duration* of private prayer (342, 343), we should recall that Ignatius had to resist pressure to extend the time to accord with earlier tradition. By fixing certain clear limits, he manifests a new understanding of the religious life. He wished the whole of life to be transformed through union with God in purity of intention (288). This union was to be lived out by means of the examen of conscience (342), which continually submitted one's actual life to enlightenment from God, and also by means of self-abnegation (307) and personal involvement through obedience (342). This was the fundamental attitude, supposedly acquired in the novitiate, that Ignatius invokes here. In the Complementary Norms (*CN* 67) the Society has discerned and spelled out what is necessary for the scholastics in order to maintain close union with God as a reality in their lives. As to the *form* of

---

[2] For a more detailed analysis of this matter, see Simon Decloux's commentary in Arzubialde, *Constituciones de la Compañía*, 155–66.

prayer, the Constitutions call for a free and simple effort to find that manner of prayer best suited to the situation of the individual and his particular needs (343).

Another Ignatian innovation in the form of the religious life is the nature and meaning of the simple vows pronounced at the conclusion of the novitiate. These vows are perpetual, but conditional. This in turn led Ignatius to introduce into the scholastic's life *the renovation of vows*, to take place twice a year (346–48). Ignatius's objective here was precise. Even if the commitment to God is perpetual on the part of the individual person, still it would be necessary to renew the memory of it and thus reinvigorate the attachment to God and affirms anew the response already made to his call. The Complementary Norms have explained and confirmed this practice (*CN* 75).

Intellectual Formation (Chapters 5–6 and 12–15)

What to study? (chapters 5 and 12)

Like everything else in the Constitutions, the material to be studied is determined by apostolic imperatives. For Ignatius the studies are never an end in themselves but are a means directly aimed at the end of the Society, helping "the souls of the members and of their neighbors" (351). Consequently, each individual's own spiritual growth and the needs of the apostolate dictate the choice of subject matter and the length of studies assigned to him. This apostolic aim is repeated once again at the beginning of chapter 12, where the discussion reaches beyond the training of Jesuits to concentrate on the Society's universities (446).

What *subjects* of study are prescribed for the Jesuit scholastics? Needless to say, we must distance ourselves from the concrete prescriptions of the Constitutions. The Complementary Norms have made the appropriate adaptations for today (*CN* 81–105). But two major themes running through this chapter remain quite applicable even if their actual implementation can take diverse forms. First of all, for everyone called to the priesthood in the Society, the apostolic and missionary ends of the Society demand a serious study of *theology* (446, 447, 450). Whoever would develop himself intellectually while neglecting theology would simply not be preparing himself for the priestly ministry of the Society. Theology is the intellectual discipline most suitable for this (446). A second theme is distinctly emphasized as twofold. The theological education of a companion presupposes a strong background in the contemporary *culture* achieved through serious study in a field of knowledge relevant to that culture. For Ignatius and his contemporaries, this usually meant literature (447, 351). Today it can mean a knowledge of and dialogue with the scientific culture, the humanities, communications, the media, and the like. This sort of formation demands as well a capacity for *philosophical* reflection on and analysis of this culture in dialogue with contemporaries. It should prepare us to deal with all the questions others bring up, even in the most fundamental areas. For Ignatius and his contemporaries, this corresponded to a study of the arts and of metaphysics (351, 450). Familiarity with the cultural realities of our own time as well as contact with current philosophical issues is a prerequisite to sound and convincing reflection on the mystery of faith. They are the seedbed from which the proclamation and the service of the faith emerge.

The Constitutions are clear enough with respect to the *doctrine* to be taught (358–59 and chap. 14). Without delaying on time-related requirements, we conclude that because the teaching of theology has an apostolic purpose in the Church, this ecclesiastical aspect is of critical importance in such a work (*CN* 99–105).

Means for learning well (chapters 6, 13, and 15)

Ignatius begins by recommending a fundamental *spiritual attitude*. Like everything else in life, one's studies should be a constituent part of the search for God and his service and glory. Hence, Ignatius first reminds the scholastics of the purity of intention with which they should order everything toward the apostolic end of the Society: the service of God and the good of souls (360–365). The "Modus Parisiensis," which placed great store by the active assimilation of knowledge, was the principal inspiration of the Jesuit *educational method*. This preference of Ignatius is scarcely astonishing, since it plays so important a role in the Spiritual Exercises, whose aim it is to discover the will of God in one's own life. Ignatius carried over into the domain of education those perspectives that he found so effective in the spiritual lives of his retreatants. After emphasizing the importance of the public lectures (369, 374), the Constitutions recommend certain specific methods: the repetitions (374, 375, 459), the disputations, which today would be called seminars (378, 380), original compositions (380, 381), study groups (383), and individual study (384).

Pastoral Formation (Chapter 8)

The very purpose of the studies dictates a gradual entry into the pastoral experience. Actually, here it is a question of gradually carrying into practice what is the very end of our vocation, just as it is of the studies we undertake. True, the text of the Constitutions suggests that for the most part this should take place near the end of studies; but today's circumstances extend it throughout the entire period of studies. We observe here that the perspective was above all else quite practical, leading to the initiation into pastoral ministry, envisioned in quite limited terms. Recent developments in the area of formation have made it desirable to extend pastoral service to other forms of service of the neighbor. The pastoral activities mentioned here in Part IV (401–14) correspond to those cited in chapter 4 of Part VII, which dealt with ways in which those in the houses and colleges should aid the neighbor. Included too are the kinds of ministry described in no. 1 of the Formula of the Institute. We point up here the importance St. Ignatius attached to teaching Christian doctrine to children and simple folk, so much so that he did not hesitate to impose this work on the rector of the college also (437), and he included it in the formula of final vows for the priests (527, 535).

In the final article of this chapter on pastoral formation (414), Ignatius lays out a broader outlook that squares exactly with the Constitutions. While preparing to enunciate some very specific criteria for activities, Master Ignatius calls us to enter upon a process of discernment and election that will take full account of the various exigencies as they arise and will open itself to guidance by the unction of the Holy Spirit.

The Financial Management of the Colleges (Chapters 2 and 11) and Their Government (Chapters 10 and 17)

St. Ignatius and the First Companions set up a type of poverty peculiar to the colleges and universities (chaps. 1, 2, and 11), and Part IV also deals with the government of these institutions (chaps. 10 and 17). But the principal treatments of poverty and governance are found in Part VI and Part IX respectively; those we will examine later. For the present, however, we underline the significance of chapter 10 in a spiritually sensitive reading of the Constitutions. The description given in Part IV, chapter 10, of the qualities expected of the rector (423) and of the role assigned to him (424), along with the portrait of the general (723–35), is among the very best images of a companion of Jesus according to the heart of Ignatius. We call attention also to the final lines of no. 424, which refer again to the obedience that Jesuit scholastics owe to the rector. Here we detect a tone quite different from the one prevalent in Part III, where the subjects discussed were novices. At this point, less emphasis is placed on exercises and ascetical practices. Now Ignatius hopes that the virtue of obedience will be more integrated, more solidified and stabilized, in this later stage of formation.

Apostolic Responsibility for Extern Students (Chapters 7, 12–15)

Part IV recommends careful selection of the extern students. Since nothing specific is said concerning their curriculum, we presume that it will be the same as that of the Jesuit scholastics. But it is specified that these externs will receive the proper Christian education, both in the colleges (395) and in the universities (481); and three requirements are spelled out to achieve this goal: First, they will be taught what pertains to the faith and Christian living; second, they will be introduced to a life of prayer and reception of the sacraments (481), but without any compulsion and with the respect due to each individual situation (482); and third, they will receive a sound moral training inspired by charity, one administered insistently but gently as well (486–89). These objectives were, of course, stated in ways adapted to the cultural context of the sixteenth century, whereas the Complementary Norms provide the directives necessary and suitable for today (277–93). Nevertheless, amid all the developments in the kinds of students Jesuit schools enroll, in the context of society, and in the actual work of education, haven't these objectives and criteria stood the test of time, and do they not still provide a sound blueprint for our apostolate in the schools or in our ministries to the young?

In the Movement toward Incorporation into the Body of the Society: One Step in the Genesis of the Group

Just as the first paragraph of no. 307 has declared, Part IV presents one step in the formation of a young Jesuit, namely, his intellectual formation. At the same time, this Part also shows how the whole Society progressively blended itself into the culture of the period and into the work of education, seeing them as means of helping souls. We are once again face to face with that developmental approach that pervades the entire Constitutions. We follow step by step the development of the candidate as he becomes a full-fledged member of the whole group, and all along we witness how the Society gradually builds itself up as a collective entity. The involvement in education and in the culture is in no sense conceived as a path to promotion or self-realization for the individual and still less for the group. The young Jesuit is urged to seek only "the glory of God and the good of souls" (360). Each individual enters with the human gifts that are his and the grace that is given him. Before him lies a path of humility leading the companion to a deeper acceptance of himself as he is (a path of personal incarnation) and of his place in the body of the Society (a path to incorporation). Thus, Part IV sets up, as it were, a permanent dimension for each of our lives as companions of Jesus. For we never quite achieve our inculturation in the world in order to proclaim and bear witness to the Gospel. Decree 4 of GC 34, "Our Mission and the Culture," forcefully summons us to this.

INTEGRATION WITH THE CULTURE: INNOVATION OR CONTINUITY?

By deciding in 1547 to accept responsibility for colleges and universities, St. Ignatius and the First Companions significantly altered their original course. When they gathered in 1537 in Venice and later in Rome, they hoped to remain free to go anywhere in the world where the pope could send them, living in total poverty and simplicity with no institutional responsibilities or cultural commitments. Only gradually did they see the need to be involved in education and cultural affairs, at first to train their own recruits but later also to "help souls." But accepting such responsibilities inevitably led to long-range involvement with the culture of the times, with contemporary society; it necessitated their entering upon the university scenes; it entailed involvement in the social and political world, the arena of politics and finance, of relationships with bishops, princes, and kings. Most of the letters of Ignatius, especially after 1547, dealt with business affairs, such as money, debts, or difficulties in reaching agreements with the founders of colleges and the like. The Society that had been so swift and mobile originally, ready to be deployed anywhere, became increasingly stable and rooted in the cities.

So there the Jesuits were—enmeshed in the world of finance, of honors, and of power. What will become of the poor and simple lifestyle described in no. 7 of the Formula, a life "more gratifying, more undefiled, and more suitable for the edification of our neighbor"? Is there a break with the original inspiration and charism? To be sure, the Society found itself at a perilous turning point in 1547. But there was no change in the purpose of the order nor in the definition of the means to be used for the care of souls. Furthermore, in the *Exposcit debitum* of 1550, fully three years after the inauguration of the first Jesuit universities, the Pope did not approve a new Society. Instead, he actually confirmed the original Formula of 1540, while being aware of the path already traveled for the last ten years. That was, in fact, the challenge and the principal function of the Constitutions, namely, to structure the body of the Society in such a way as to integrate certain institutional and cultural choices of means without risking the identity or the charism of the original small band. It was important to discover just "how the whole body of the Society could be preserved and increased in its well-being" (title of Part X). For in this Part X—the final and shortest in the Constitutions, but also the most important, because it penetrates to the very essence— Ignatius insists first of all on placing our confidence in Christ alone (812), to live just as he had always done from the time of his pilgrimage to Jerusalem thirty-five years earlier. In those days, the young convert had refused all human assistance in order to practice this confidence in God alone (*PilgTest* 35, 44). Now in composing the Constitutions, he makes "natural means" and human involvement part and parcel of them. It is an immense challenge. There is always the risk of being absorbed by these very human involvements and by the surrounding culture, while losing sight of the Society's purpose, which is "to help souls for the glory and praise of God." What were the steps taken by Ignatius to fend off these dangers? Against the lure of money, a vow of absolute poverty (816, 553); against possible ambition, a vow to renounce all ecclesiastical honors (817); against the desire for power, a theology-inspired obedience making one consider himself always as an instrument sent by Christ through his delegate (821, 547). André Ravier has some interesting pages on this subject. To quote from him,

> Ignatius strove to maintain the original ideal of the "pilgrim" throughout these changing conditions of life and activities. The entire body of the Society, like each individual member, will essentially remain a pilgrim of Christ. Only a complete break will grow into an intimate detachment rather than one that is exterior and spectacular.[3]

---

[3] Ravier, *Ignatius*, 399. For more on how the practical formation in the Society is carried out in the various stages in today's Society, see the following comments of Fr. Kolvenbach: "Some Aspects of Formation: From the End of the Novitiate to the Beginning of Regency," *Acta Romana* 20, no. 1 (1988): 85–106; "Regency as a Step in Formation," *Acta Romana* 20, no. 3 (1990): 362–76; "Special Studies," *Acta Romana* 20, no. 5 (1992): 737–44; "Directives regarding Tertianship," *Acta Romana* 20, no. 4 (1991): 621–31. All these documents are in French.

Part V: Admission and Incorporation into the Society

Part V · · · · · ·

ADMISSION OR INCORPORATION INTO THE SOCIETY

THEME OF PART V

Having covered the different stages of the candidate's formation (Examen and Parts I to IV), Ignatius, always remaining faithful to the developmental structure that he imprinted on the Constitutions, arrives at the "incorporation into the Society of those who have been formed" (137). Except for Part X, this Part V is the shortest of the Constitutions; however, in the mind of its author it is closely linked to Part VI, which concerns the life of the fully incorporated member. Already in the general plan of the Constitutions, the word "incorporation" occurs in the title of both these parts. This emphasizes that the reality of incorporation is more than simply a momentary event in the development of the Jesuit (Part V), but rather a new and substantive element in his very existence as a companion of Jesus (Part VI). The candidate becomes a fully integrated member of the Society according to the grace of his particular vocation "to live and die in it for the greater glory of God" (51, 102, 119, 126, 193, 336, 511).

It is interesting to note that in text *B* of the Constitutions, which is the Spanish version completed in 1556 and annotated by Ignatius toward the end of his life, the title of this Part is "Admission or Incorporation into the Society." One would be tempted to regard these as synonyms; but the official Latin translation of 1590, reproduced in the most recent Latin edition (1995), along with the Complementary Norms, ruled out this interpretation. Now, *to admit* someone into an institute can suggest a primarily administrative and bureaucratic action, while *to incorporate* expresses the existential fact that one has become a member of a living body. Since such a significant nuance would undoubtedly have been in the mind of Ignatius, who spoke so often of the "body of the Society," the word "incorporation" was almost certainly added in the title as a synonym that more explicitly expresses the full meaning of final *admission* of the candidate into the Society.

PLACEMENT AND PLAN OF PART V IN THE CONSTITUTIONS

Part V in the Developmental Structure of the Constitutions

From the beginning of the Constitutions, we have followed the stages or moments in the individual Jesuit's progress that are also to remain substantial and permanent elements in his life as a Jesuit. These different moments have a historic background and also enunciate a new element that will persist. The Jesuit who, possibly during his tertianship, reflects on the various stages in his formation will recognize certain characteristics that remain in his life even today. All the foregoing experiences prepared for the moment of admission by means of final vows, which fully integrate the companion into the body of the Society; and this full incorporation will also remain a permanent and constitutive element of his life. We can say that this gradual integration reflects that dynamic of progress running through the entire Constitutions. But the word "progress" is paradoxical, for it does not denote the progress of success in a strictly human enterprise. It is not a question of climbing ever higher, but rather of descending and plunging oneself more deeply into what is real. At every step in his formation, the companion is urged, on the one hand, to enter upon a path of incarnation reaching into the depths of his being, with all his gifts as well as his limitations. On the other hand, he is also challenged to follow a road leading progressively toward incorporation and assimilation into the body of the Society. With his last vows, he will complete this process of incorporation, taking his place in a united body of diverse members—a unique yet limited place, for he will be only a single member of a varied group.

The spiritual wisdom of St. Ignatius, written into the Constitutions, consists in awakening in the candidate a keen desire for spiritual and personal progress. This desire will continue to be fostered and respected. At the same time, the candidate will be gently led back down to earth, toward realizing and accepting himself as he really is. And this occurs through the discovery of what use he has made of his own gifts and abilities, along with an acceptance of his objective limits. This is a realistic way of living the colloquy of the Standards. For it is the strong desire for attachment to Christ, the poor and humble servant, that is the engine of this "progress" in the paradoxical Ignatian sense of the term. Cultivation of this Ignatian dynamic of desire right up to definitive incorporation helps to avoid those disappointments and misunderstandings often arising out of unfulfilled dreams and unrealized personal projects, and out of a lack of self-knowledge. This is the secret of that joy which characterizes someone who is happy and secure in his proper situation within the Society (111, 117, 132, and so forth). Fr. Kolvenbach has written that "the Jesuit in formation is called gradually to become what God expects of him in accordance with the vocation received: an apostle in the service of the Lord and his Church—and, if he is a scholastic, a priest of Jesus Christ—through membership in the Society of Jesus."[1]

Part V Illumined by the Spiritual Exercises

There are different ways of interpreting the dynamic at work in the Constitutions. From the Preamble on, we have given special emphasis to a dynamism revealing, one after the other, the stages of each companion's Jesuit development and demonstrating how they parallel the origin and early progress of the entire body of the Society. Keeping this fundamental perspective before us, we can detect in the Constitutions a dynamic similar to that of the Spiritual Exercises. In this light,

---

[1] "Some Aspects of Formation," 89.

the Examen and Parts I–V, treating the formation of the individual, can be compared to the first two Weeks of the Exercises, which serve to lead to an interior knowledge of Christ, the better to love and serve him (*SpEx* 104). Formation is like a practical daily implementation of the process shown in the Exercises. Part V, dealing with definitive incorporation through the vows, corresponds to the Election, while Parts VI to X, which concern the life of the companion fully formed and the Society's mission in the Church, Christ's Mystical Body, can be clarified by the contemplation of the paschal mystery in the Third and Fourth Weeks. After celebrating the Eucharist—an election that encompasses all our elections—Jesus accomplished the mission given him by the Father by handing over his life to the very end in order to gather the straying children of God.

Like the Election of the Exercises, Part V is the turning point in the dynamic of the Constitutions. In the Exercises, the Election is a free act by which a human being enters into an alliance with God, applying a specific meaning to his life in response to a call received. In a manner entirely analogous, by freely accepting a call, lived out by professing the vows, the Jesuit makes a permanent and definitive commitment to incorporation in the Society in the grade assigned him in the body of that group, in order to work in the vineyard of the Lord (Part VII) and to care for the union and welfare of the part of Christ's Mystical Body that is the Society.

The Plan of Part V

This plan is extremely simple and similar to that of Parts I and II. After providing a résumé of the various types of membership in the Society,[2] Ignatius begins by indicating those authorized to admit to final vows and the point at which this should be done (chap. 1). He then lists the qualities expected of those who will be admitted (chap. 2). Finally, he describes the procedures to be followed. As in the case of Parts I and II, the plan is relational, concentrating first on the one who admits or receives and then moving on to the one who is received. Finally he focuses attention on criteria to be applied and the attendant circumstances to be sought, all lived entirely as a prayer to

---

[2] See also *CN* 6.

God. To be incorporated into the Society is to enter into a living body and thus into a network of relationships to be experienced with confidence. Surprisingly, we use the word "admission" although we are speaking of companions who very often have spent fifteen or even twenty years in the Society, yet another indication that admission is a progressive and gradual phenomenon. We simply point out here that this final admission is not to probation, but to full incorporation.[3]

THE UNITY AND DIVERSITY OF INCORPORATION (CHAPTER 1)

Fundamental Inspiration

An understanding of Part V requires a thorough knowledge of the first paragraph (510) and declaration *A* (511) of chapter 1. Here we have a comprehensive view of Ignatius's understanding of admission and incorporation, as well as a panoramic synopsis of the entire group and its different members. At the outset Ignatius stipulates in no. 510 that the probationary period should be long enough for the two parties— the Society and the candidate requesting admission—to become sufficiently acquainted. Only then will it be possible to discern whether or not it will be conducive to God's greater glory and to the progress of souls for the candidate to become a full member. But once adequate time has elapsed, the candidate will be fully admitted and incorporated as a member of the Society. In no. 510 Ignatius stresses the unity of the group. In the declaration that follows (511), however, he reviews the different kinds and degrees of membership. Ignatius always laid great emphasis on the different types of vocation to the Society. His regard for the diversity of graces is evident in the very first paragraph of the 1540 Formula, composed well before there was any question of fixed or juridical grades. Respecting and accommodating this variety of graces and gifts from God, Ignatius did not want incorporation to be rigidly uniform. He was pleased by the diversity of the Society's membership and sought

---

[3] See the title of Part I and no. 202; see also the title of Part V.

to integrate into one apostolic body men who had responded differently to different vocations from the Lord. This is the inspiration behind the grades in the Society: to honor the diversity of God's gifts and to recognize this diversity itself as a grace.[4]

The Different Grades: Origin and Development

Ignatius never had a predetermined plan to guide him as he founded the Society. He simply allowed the Holy Spirit to lead him step by step, as the early history bears witness. "He was gently led whither he did not know," as Nadal testifies. It follows that the qualities required for the profession and therefore the different categories of membership that eventually developed in the Society were not part of a preordained schema, but grew out of experience and concrete circumstances. When analyzing the early stages of the Examen, we noted how the general idea of coadjutors, both priests and brothers, originated. Moreover, Ignatius came progressively to understand the need not only for holiness of life but also for adequate theological learning in order to implement the missions assigned by the Sovereign Pontiff. This development can be verified by comparing no. 9 of the Formula of 1540 with that of 1550. In 1540 the criteria for profession were learning *or* holiness; by 1550, the "or" had changed to "and": "[They are] conspicuous in the integrity of Christian life and learning." However, when zealous priests of virtue and piety, but with limited theological knowledge, asked to join the group, Ignatius sought to include them while respecting their own graces and recognizing their gifts and limitations. They would not personally pronounce the vow of obedience to the pope for the missions, and would therefore remain more readily available to serve the internal needs of the Society and its regular priestly ministries. These are the "spiritual coadjutors." In a similar manner, Ignatius would also receive lay persons who offered themselves to aid the Society in tasks not directly sacerdotal. Then designated "temporal coadjutors," they are now called by the beautiful name "brothers." As

---

[4] Peter-Hans Kolvenbach, S.J., "La Vocation et la mission du frère jesuite," *CIS* 78 (1995): 13.

we have observed in our study of the Examen, the idea of these different forms of incorporation came to maturity in 1546 and was approved by the Pope in the brief *Exponi nobis.*

The introduction of scholastics followed a similar pattern. As early as 1539, Ignatius and his companions realized that it was unrealistic to hope to rely exclusively on recruits who had already completed their education. Early on in Part IV (308), they record how they confronted this problem and decided "to take another path, that of admitting young men" whose studies they would subsidize This was covered already in the 1540 Formula of the Institute (*FI* 8). Around this time a group of young students who were candidates for the Society departed for study in Paris after promising to enter the Society at an appropriate time. After a period of experimentation, they also took the three vows, again with a promise to enter the Society. The Formula of 1550 mentions them in no. 9 after the professed and the coadjutors as members of the Society, though not yet fully incorporated into it.

Little by little, thanks to experience, reflection, and frequent reconsideration of the question in prayer, St. Ignatius came to define the body of the Society: It would be composed of a number of members in different categories, but organically united by the desire and the shared determination to work toward the end and purpose of the Society, to recall the description found in no. 511. Everyone is fully a member, but each according to the grace of his vocation and his personal gifts. The scholastics are simply approved, the coadjutors are formed, and the others are professed. All participate in the unique vocation of the Society, but in different ways, each one according to his calling and his position in the group. In particular, all share in the priestly mission of the Society, for the activity of everyone, even if he is not himself a priest, is more than just parallel to that of the priests. It is always closely directed toward achieving the sacerdotal purpose that activates and energizes the whole Society.

In his article on the brothers' vocation cited earlier, while discussing the origin of the coadjutors, Fr. Kolvenbach demonstrates that Ignatius did not recruit priests and brothers for practical reasons.[5] Rather he received those sent by the Lord who had infused into their hearts a passionate desire to help people encounter Christ and to participate, each in his own way, in the enterprise of the First Companions to aid others to encounter the Lord. Unless we retain this perspective of faith, we can never experience the fraternal companionship of friends in the Lord. All the services and ministries of Jesuits have the same evangelical value. In the Society there are only servants at work for the Kingdom.

THE QUALITIES OF THOSE WHO ARE ADMITTED (CHAPTER 2)

Basically Ignatius prescribed the same qualities for all the candidates (516, 522, 524). But these qualities will be required in different proportions for the different grades. A comparison of texts *a* or *A* (1550) with text *B* (1556) shows that in text *B* Ignatius was explicit about intellectual competence for the professed (518), while retaining the same spiritual standards for all. These spiritual qualities are spelled out in no. 516, which describes what Ignatius calls the "school of the heart." This text is among the founder's most inspiring portraits of what he hoped the companion of Jesus would be. At the same time, it also summarizes what he wanted to accomplish in the greatest measure possible in the tertianship experience. For him every Jesuit is called to become the kind of man described here. In this sense, therefore, Ignatius looks to find the same qualities in every Jesuit in every grade, always in proportion to the grace given him. That is why, during this last year of probation, every Jesuit must be formed in the school of the heart. The Complementary Norms stressed this point (125–27) by including the brothers, who were not held to this norm in earlier centuries, given the cultural milieu of Ignatius's time. In view of the fundamental and practical equality of spiritual gifts envisioned for everyone, in proportion to each one's grace, the

---

[5] See n. 4 above.

differences will be tied to the diversity of particular vocations and grades to which each one will be called within the one body of the Society of Jesus. The Complementary Norms spell out the different criteria for admission to final vows (*CN* 118–24).

INCORPORATION THROUGH THE VOWS (CHAPTERS 3 AND 4)

Chapters 3 and 4 describe the procedures for admitting to final incorporation in the Society of Jesus. Although quite juridical on the surface, they do, however, contain the four formulas of the vows, the only prayers in the entire text of the Constitutions. They contribute a certain personal and relational atmosphere to this chapter, one that reaches beyond the necessary juridical content. For the individual Jesuit it is, after all, the offering of himself to God and his Christ by means of this integration into the Society. It is worthwhile to meditate on the formulas. The one appointed for the scholastics is especially charged with spiritual meaning. The whole unfolding of the Exercises is recaptured there as if to revitalize in the heart of the young Jesuit that fundamental conversion which prepares for his incorporation into the Society.

Incorporation through the Vows

We must note here that it is by pronouncing the vows that the Jesuit is incorporated into the Society. The Society recognizes that God is the source of every vocation and of the Society itself (134, 812). The desire of the individual member, which has grown and matured, is secondary; it finds its source in God. And the Society, within whose social structure this desire has been molded and channeled, is itself secondary. The Society comes from God and is continually reborn of God through the covenant that he fashions in Christ with each member of his body.

The Meaning of the Vow

The vow is the consecration of one's whole being to God. This consecration itself is the covenant that Christ makes with the companion, who is thereby introduced to a particular and more interior form of that intimacy with Christ first initiated in baptism. Our consecration and thus also our vows are second-ary; that is, they are responses to God's initiative involving free acceptance of his gift and of his invitation. In Part III (282–83), Ignatius had already stressed with some vigor this response to God's gift and will return to it again in no. 544. This introduction by means of the vows into a new intimacy with the Lord is at the same time a visible and outward expression of our membership in the body of Christ that is the Church and of our commitment within the Church to the Society of Jesus.[6]

The Meaning of the Vows Pronounced before the Body of Christ

Reflecting the diversity in their spiritual traditions, religious orders have different rituals for the ceremony of the vows. Moreover, in the aftermath of the Second Vatican Council, a rite of profession was proposed, to be placed at the end of the Liturgy of the Word. But Ignatius and the First Companions spontaneously pronounced their vows in an original manner both on August 15, 1534, at Montmartre and on April 22, 1541, at St. Paul's outside the Walls. As they put it, they took these vows in the presence of "the Body of Christ" just as we still do today.[7] They wanted to express by a visible and outward sign the total gift of themselves as companions responding with complete confidence to the Lord's total gift of himself. As is evident from the description of the rite given in no. 525, the profession is made to Christ himself, Almighty God, really present in the Host, which is visible to the companion as he reads his vows. The Communion that follows immediately is a ratification by Christ of the commitment that the candidate has made to him. This manner of celebrating the vows exhibits certain traits characteristic of Ignatian spirituality:

▸ The insistence on the offering of oneself (annotation 5 of the Exercises) and on the exchange of love and of gifts (*SpEx* 234; see also the colloquy to Christ in the First Week, *SpEx* 53);

---

[6] See *Lumen gentium*, 43–47.

[7] Peter-Hans Kolvenbach, S.J., Letter "On the 450th Anniversary of the Vows of Montmartre," *Acta Romana* 19, no. 1 (1988): 80–83.

> ▸ The mysteries of the Incarnation, the Eucharist, and the Passion contemplated as proofs of love (*SpEx* 289), with the word "sacrifice" being more apt than "sacrament" to describe an action;

> ▸ Perpetual vows understood as the ideal way to unite oneself to God and to exercise one's freedom with respect to him (283);

> ▸ The manner in which the pilgrim at Manresa was pleased to effect a union with the Eucharist by meditating on the Passion, as well as his lifelong mystical experiences while celebrating the Eucharist.[8]

The vows pronounced "before the Body of Christ" emphasize the connection between the Eucharistic Body of Christ and his Mystical Body, into which Jesuits are concretely incorporated through the body of the Society. By the vows pronounced at Montmartre, according to Fr. Kolvenbach, an apostolic community came into being from the Eucharist, as did a declaration of a paschal love lived out through apostolic ministries freely rendered. Noelle Hausman remarked that "the Ignatian practice highlights the missionary dynamic issuing from the vow to undertake a pilgrimage, a vow that is constitutive of the Society of Jesus."[9]

The Vows of Coadjutors and Scholastics

The simple vows of the coadjutors were a novelty in Ignatius's time; before that, all the vows were solemn. Even more surprising, while these vows were public and perpetual, they were also conditional.[10] These innovations have often been victims of misunderstanding and criticism, especially as regards the conditional nature of the vows, as if this arrangement were somehow selfish and looked only to the advantage of the Society. Quite to the contrary, however, Ignatius was concerned for the welfare of the members themselves. In those days solemn

---

[8] These reflections were inspired by a handwritten note of Father L. Renard, S.J.

[9] Noelle Hausmann, "Pour La Profession super hostiam: Une etude de la profession religieuse," *Nouvelle Revue Théologique* 110 (1988): 729–42.

[10] See *FI* 9 and *Cons* 534 and 536.

vows were never dispensed, so that someone who left a religious order remained bound by the vows. By contrast, a religious in simple, conditional vows ceased to be bound by the vows upon leaving the religious order. To be sure, dispensation from the vows is now granted by the Holy See if the reasons are sound. During the Thirty-fourth General Congregation, however, the Pope asked the Society not to discuss the possibility of making all the Jesuit vows solemn, a change that would require an alteration in the text of the Formula of the Institute.[11]

The vows of the scholastics also have their unique features. First of all, they are addressed directly to the "almighty and eternal God," with no mention of the superior of the Society. At this stage the Society is primarily a witness to the commitment and will accompany the member during the long period of growth between the first and the last vows. When the time for last vows arrives, the body of the Society receives the vows through the superior and for its own part confirms its commitment to the individual. This way of proceeding was unknown before the time of Ignatius, when solemn vows were taken immediately after the novitiate. Furthermore, the simple vows of the scholastics and the younger brothers were, like those of the formed coadjutors, perpetual but conditional. This can more easily be understood in their case, for this kind of vow is more appropriate during the long period between the novitiate and definitive incorporation into the Institute. It is true that today in the majority of institutes temporary but renewable vows are the norm. But this solution has the disadvantage of suggesting a consecration to the Lord that is limited in time. It conflicts with the deep longing of the person who truly offers himself to God; true love does not admit of such limitations. The manner of proceeding proposed by Ignatius respects the desire of the young religious to give himself without reservation. At the same time, it permits the Society to dissolve the first vows if serious and proportionate reasons arise.

---

[11] See the letter of Father General in *Acta Romana* 21, no. 1 (1994): 52–53.

Certain Other Matters regarding the Vows

▸ The vow of obedience to the pope concerning missions is discussed in nos. 529 and especially 605.

▸ The promise made by all Jesuit priests to teach Christian doctrine to children and simple people is clarified in no. 528.

▸ The content of the five simple vows of the professed is set forth more explicitly in the Complementary Norms (*CN* 134–42).

▸ The significance of the final vows in the Society is explained by Fr. Michael Buckley in a text quoted at the end of this chapter, on pages 91-94.

▸ The practical preparations and procedures to be made at the time of last vows are described in the booklet entitled *Practica quædam.*[12]

MODERN PROBLEMS REGARDING THE GRADES AND THE FOURTH VOW

Grades in the Body of the Society

The different grades and the complexity within the body of the Society, as described at the beginning of Part V (511) and in the Formula of 1550 (*FI* 9), have caused debates and tensions throughout these four and one-half centuries of history. Does this image of the Society really reflect the serious intentions of Ignatius, or was it a transitory situation intended to disappear once there were enough professed fathers to render the aid of spiritual coadjutors superfluous? That is the view of Fr. Ladislas Lukács in an article published over thirty years ago in the *Archivum historicum Societatis Iesu.*[13] Others, however, maintain that we have in no. 511 Ignatius's final description of membership in the Society, an understanding that he developed "little by little through experience and reflection, made under the influence of the grace that he constantly begged for in

---

[12] (Rome: General Curia S.J., 1991), 29–38.

[13] "De graduum diverstate inter sacerdotes in Societate Iesu," *Archivum historicum Societatis Iesu* 36 (1968): 237–316.

prayer." This is the position taken by Fr. Paulo Dezza in his article "The Members of the Society."[14] It is likewise the opinion of Fr. Antonio de Aldama.[15] Truly, it is difficult to interpret the mind of Ignatius by referring to his practice, which seems at times disconcerting.[16]

Clearly, interpretations of the Ignatian criteria governing incorporation into the Society have led to tension, misunderstanding, and even bitterness throughout our history. During the generalate of Claudio Aquaviva, toward the end of the sixteenth century, 42 percent of the priests were spiritual coadjutors, but by the suppression in 1773 this grade accounted for no more than 5 percent. After the restoration, between 1829 and 1964 the spiritual coadjutors climbed to 60 percent of the priests in the Society. It is difficult to understand just what were the reasons for these notable divergences. In his report on the state of the Society during the congregation of provincials in 1990, Fr. Kolvenbach showed how widely the criteria for last vows differ today among the provinces and among the assistancies.[17]

It seems likely that soon after the death of St. Ignatius, the doctrinal requirements for the profession of four vows were overemphasized and interpreted with excessive rigidity. Perhaps the intention was to preserve what was deemed a substantial of our Institute. But the criteria came to concentrate too exclusively on intellectual and scholarly attainments and were too often applied in a manner that was hardly satisfactory. Indeed, it was not rare for some coadjutors to prove more effective in the apostolate than many of the professed. Questions about this have been raised for centuries, but especially in more recent years since GC 31.

---

[14] This article is found in *The Formula of the Institute,* CIS (Rome, 1982).

[15] De coadjutoribus Societatis Jesu in mente et in praxi Sancti," *Archivum historicum Societatis Iesu* 37 (1969): 389–430.

[16] See Ravier, *Ignatius,* 378–86, 526–28.

[17] See the address of Fr. General "On the State of the Society," *Acta Romana* 20, no. 3 (1990): 484.

The Thirty-First General Congregation (1965–1966)

During this general congregation, questions regarding the requirements for profession and the manner in which they had been implemented were confronted and adjustments were made more in harmony with modern times. The congregation issued good replies touching on the criteria for admission to last vows. In particular, it gave attention to what was meant by "a sufficient knowledge of doctrine." It should no longer be tied exclusively to success in the examination *ad gradum*.[18] In addition, the same congregation promulgated an important decree on the brothers (decree 7), stressing the participation of all, priests and brothers, in the one apostolic vocation in the one priestly Society.

Still, a much more basic question had arisen: the very existence of grades among the formed members of the Society. The question arose especially because Vatican Council II was about to ratify *Perfectæ caritatis*, the decree that called for the suppression within religious communities of all distinctions that did not stem from priestly ordination. After deliberating at considerable length, the congregation decided that the state of the question was insufficiently clear. It therefore called for a commission to be formed that could study the matter and report to the next general congregation.[19]

The Thirty-Second General Congregation (1974–1975)

Many *postulata* on the subject of grades and their suppression were sent to this congregation, convened by Fr. Arrupe on December 3, 1974. Fifty-eight of these *postulata* came from provincial congregations. This seemed to indicate that the majority of provinces desired the suppression of these grades. But at the same time, in a letter from the Vatican Secretary of

---

[18] With this understanding, as spelled out in *CN* 120–122, we must read GC 31, d. 11, nos. 4 and 5 (marginal nos. 197 and 198). The decrees of GC 31 and 32 are recorded in *Documents of the 31st and 32nd General Congregations of the Society of Jesus* (St. Louis: Institute of Jesuit Sources, 1977). All further references to these decrees will make use of this source.

[19] See GC 31, d. 5.

State to Fr. General on December 3, Pope Paul VI made it known that any proposed extension of the fourth vow to all Jesuits, even those not ordained, would pose grave obstacles to the Holy See's giving the necessary approval.

The members of the congregation believed, nevertheless, that they could still make a "representation" to the Pope, a step that would be normal enough according to the Ignatian concept of obedience. Hence, there was a lengthy discussion in the congregation during which the advantages and the disadvantages of suppressing the grades—so that all Jesuits would pronounce the same four vows—were fully explored. The indicative or provisional vote that followed showed a large majority in favor of suppressing the distinction. The congregation thereupon communicated this result to the Holy See as a representation in the Ignatian sense of the term, meant to acquaint the Pope with its thinking on this subject. In an autograph letter of February 15, 1975, the Pope informed the congregation that it had acted against his wishes and ordered that the subject be pursued no further. As the final and supreme guarantor of the essentials of the Institute, he could not accede to any change in this matter at all.[20] There had been a serious misunderstanding between the Pope and the congregation, who had believed that a representation was still possible, especially considering the apparent nuances in the first letter of December 2, 1974. But after receiving the autograph letter, the congregation accepted the decision of the Pope in a spirit of fidelity and obedience. Since then the question of grades has not been treated. During the preparations for the Thirty-fourth Congregation, Pope John Paul II clearly expressed a desire that this subject not be introduced.

The Current Situation

We can say, first of all, that the new criteria and methods adopted by the Thirty-first General Congregation and included in the Complementary Norms (*CN* 118–24) regulating admis-

---

[20] See GC 32, d. 8, and its historical preface, pp. 373–75.

sion to last vows are well adapted to the situation today.[21] But what is to be said about the suppression of the grades and about having all the members, brothers as well as priests, pronounce the fourth vow of obedience to the pope with respect to missions? Although distinct, the two questions are interrelated. Here is not the place to enter into a detailed examination of this complex problem; rather, we will offer some facts to ponder, without prejudice to the opinion of the Holy See.

Recent general congregations have moved toward the suppression of grades largely because, as culture and mentalities have developed, there is a longing for equality and fraternity, a viewpoint, in any case, confirmed by Vatican II in *Perfectæ caritatis*. But such a change could be envisaged and effected at various levels.

▸ On one level, all the priests could make the profession of the four vows and the grade of spiritual coadjutor would gradually disappear. One must recognize that this would ratify a prevailing trend, since it is obvious that in several provinces nearly all the priests are called to the profession. But shouldn't the possible effects of this change on the long-term welfare of the Society be pondered at the outset, and shouldn't measures be taken in this regard to avoid any damage that might ensue?

▸ On another level, the suppression of grades would include the extension of the fourth vow to all the members, priests and brothers alike. This was the preference, it seems, of the members at GC 32 in 1975. But does this proposal take sufficient account of what this vow of obedience to the pope concerning the missions actually means? More precisely, is not ordination to the priesthood a necessary prerequisite for taking this vow? This is not because the vow is some kind of privilege, but rather because ordination is bound up with the very nature of the vow. This is the opinion of a certain number of theologians.[22]

---

[21] GC 31, d. 11.

[22] A. Chapelle "Le Quatrième Voeu dans la Compagnie, *CIS* (1978).

Even granting its juridical dimension, the vow does in the truest sense of the term impinge on the very essence of a person, placing him in an ontologically new situation before God and before other persons. This is true of the three vows of religion and also of the vow of obedience to the pope with regard to missions. This latter vow, however, has a very precise object plainly specified in Part V (529) and in no. 3 of the Formula as well. It binds the Jesuit to the pope for the accomplishment of the universal Church's mission, which is "the welfare of souls and the propagation of the faith." This mission of the Church, which continues that of Jesus, is essentially a sacerdotal mission that cannot, therefore, be accomplished in its sacramental totality except by an ordained priest. This argument has weight and should be considered and evaluated, I believe, in any reflection on the eventual admission of all the companions to the fourth vow. If the argument is valid and just, what sense would it make to propose this vow to someone who is not ordained a priest?

To conclude the discussion, this complex question of the grades and of the fourth vow must in due time become the subject of a genuine spiritual discernment, since there will always be strong arguments both for and against each of the possible options. The important thing is to seek and find the will of God for the Society and to follow the path along which the Holy Spirit wishes to conduct us. Obviously, this search itself should be undertaken in a spirit of docility and obedience to the Vicar of Christ, to whom the entire Society is bound by this special vow as a visible sign of our union with Christ.[23]

Note concerning the Vow of Obedience to the Pope

The significance of the "fourth vow" has been much enhanced during the tertianship by reading the Formula of the Institute" (345). As John Paul II has himself declared in his

---

[23] See the address of Paul VI to GC 32, in *Documents of the 31st and 32nd General Congregations,* 519–36. More details are found in the article discussing Part V written by Carlos Soltero, S.J., in *Incorporation of a Spirit,* 225–52.

encyclical *Ut unum sint* (1995), treating ecumenical endeavors, fidelity to the vow calls for an effort to find the most appropriate way of living out this close bond with the universal Church, of which the pope is the servant of unity in faith and in community. It is helpful to read the final allocutions of Fr. Kolvenbach to the provincials and to the procurators, as well as decree 11 of GC 34 on the attitude of service within the bosom of the Church.[24]

Here we cite at length an essay, somewhat edited, of Fr. Michael J. Buckley, S.J., that seems apposite here.

FINAL VOWS: CULMINATION
OF AN IGNATIAN "ELECTION"

So many Jesuits have asked what it means to take final vows in the Society. After the novitiate, they had already pronounced their vows and over the years have repeated them "not to take on a new obligation, but to remind themselves of the one they already have in the Lord and to confirm it" (*Cons.* 544).

It makes little sense, it would seem, to take "final" vows when the ones which have been so often pronounced are perpetual. How much more final can you get than perpetual? There is no religious order except the Society of Jesus which takes perpetual vows so early and final vows so late!

To understand the meaning of final vows, it is necessary to place them within the general structure of an Ignatian election, the way in which one moves toward finding and giving his life over to the will of God. There is the initial offer of a choice to God our Lord, an offering that is made according to a time for making an election and which is then presented before the Lord.

Ignatius indicates the various ways in which this can be done in the Exercises and embodies this method of election, along with its offering in his deliberations on poverty, preserved in his *Spiritual Journal*. What the dynamic of the election looks for after the moment of offering is the subsequent confirmation by God. Election as a religious history, as an experience of Providence, develops over time between these two major events: the time of human offering and the period of confirmation by God.

---

[24] *Acta Romana* 20, no. 3 (1990): 491–506, especially nos. 18–21; ibid., 19, no. 4 (1987): 1078–90, especially numbers 6–9.

The vows of the Society follow a similar pattern. The first vows of a Jesuit are an offering, following upon an election, made in perpetuity, very much like the initial election of the Exercises. Like this offering, they are contingent upon the subsequent confirmation by the Lord, worked through a human being's personal religious history over the next ten or fifteen years. These first vows can and do have two possible and quite legitimate fulfillments: last vows or dismissal.

No Dispensation Needed

If the initial offering of a man's life through first vows is not confirmed by God acting through his Church, the person should be dismissed from the Society. This is the reason why if a man is dismissed after first vows (only), he is not dispensed from these vows. They have reached one of the two natural terms, in this case in dismissal.

When those in first vows are dismissed, they leave the Society of Jesus "per modum exclusionis," i.e., in a manner similar to those who, for example, have taken vows for a three-year period and at the completion of that period have not been allowed to renew them. There is no dispensation from these vows; the period of their existence has reached its natural termination.

In sharp contrast, the dismissal of those in final simple vows is "per viam dismissionis" and must be accompanied, as is the case, by an ipso facto dissolution of these vows or otherwise they would still obtain.[25]

Witness Is Ratified

If the religious experience and history of the young Jesuit witness the confirmation of his initial offering, then the Society calls him to pronounce last vows—the Society witnesses that the initial offering of so many years before has been accepted and confirmed by God.

That is the reason why the situation of last vows is, in so many ways, so different. It is much more an act of God confirming the initial offering than a new offering. First vows are made only to God—read over the vow formula and notice that no human person is addressed. They are an offering to God to live and to die as a Jesuit.

---

[25] See "De valore votorum post noviciatum in Societate et de eorum solutione," a rescript from the Sacred Congregation of Religious, August 10, 1959, *Acta Romana* 13 (1956–60): 577.

Last vows, in contrast, are commitments made not only to God, but to the Society—compare the two different formulae from the Constitutions, no. 527, in contrast with nos. 539–40. Last vows, unlike first, are accepted by the Society, as the man "vows into the hands of the one who admits them" (533), and they are as serious and solemn a confirmation of religious and personal choice of a way of life as this Church can give.

Up until this time, the Jesuit lives in a period of probation, testing whether the first offering of his life to God in this way is accepted and confirmed by divine providence.

What is that confirmation? Years, many years, have passed since the young man with the promise and the optimism of the young entered the novitiate. Over that history, he has experienced in some depth the fulfillment and the searing disappointments of that promise.

He has known weakness, self-doubt, frustrated expectations. And the easy optimism that goes with being young has yielded much more to hope, a hope in what he does not see:

"And what you thought you came for is only a shell, a husk of meaning from which the purpose breaks only when it is fulfilled, if at all. Either you had no purpose or the purpose is beyond the end you figured, and is altered in fulfillment."[26]

When a man comes to last vows, he knows—as only extended, day by day experience can teach—what it will mean for him to live a life of fidelity in the poverty, chastity, and obedience of the Society of Jesus.

He knows, as only living in various communities can instill, who the Society of Jesus is, the men with whom he will spend his life. It is a very different person whom the Society calls to last vows.

Yet over the immense changes of those years, the happiness and the struggle through which he has moved, the offering has remained—deepened, differently modulated, but persistent. The confirmation of God runs through this history and is embodied in his knowing choice of these men as his brothers and this way of life as his path to God.

What is this confirmation? These years have been spent in the various houses, at the various tasks and missions of the Society. And the Society—concrete, flawed, intense, needing the mercy of God—recognizes in him the persistent presence of its charism, the constella-

---

[26] T. S. Eliot, "Little Gidding," *Four Quartets* (London: Faber and Faber, 1945.

tion of graces that it calls vocation. The men of the Society find in him a brother, possessed by a common apostolic dedication.

A Mutual Recognition

They have lived a common history together, and the steadiness of his desire has been matched by this common recognition of the vocation of his life. He is among those whom Ignatius soberly describes as "those who have been tested in the Society sufficiently and for a time long enough so that both parties may know whether their remaining in it is conducive to the greater service and glory of God our Lord" (510).

Last vows are not a technical refinement. To miss the distinction between first and last vows is to miss the fundamental religious providence which they embody, the way that a Jesuit searches out the divine will in his life, the movement between choice and its acceptance by God, the time that must be lived between the election and the confirmation.

The offering of the novice is important and an enormous gift of God, and he promises with these to enter the Society when the Society will call him. The confirmation of last vows, in a formula that is far more laconic, is much more the action of God, taking up what has been given so many years before and asserting that it is His.

Ignatius was of the opinion that a human being could find the divine will in his life through the process of offering and confirmation. The vows of the Society are structured on that conviction, moving over a history from first vows to last vows "to find the divine will in the disposition of my entire life" (*SpEx* 1).[27]

---

[27] Reprinted by permission from the *National Jesuit News* (April 1981), 8 and 10.

PART VI: THE PERSONAL LIFE OF THOSE ALREADY ADMITTED AND INCORPORATED

(Outline of Text *B* and Comparison with Texts *a* and *A*)

Texts a and A	Text *B*
III	**Chap. 1: What pertains to obedience (547–52):**
	1. Chastity (542.2)
	2. Obedience (547, §3–552)
	holy obedience: fundamental principle, spirit, scope, manner (547–50)
	relation to the superior
	love and respect; manifestation of conscience, (551)
	having recourse to him (552)
I	**Chap. 2: What pertains to poverty (553–81)**
	1. A firm wall (553–54): to love it, fidelity to the Founders, a special vow
	2. Community poverty (555–69)
	to accept no fixed revenues (555–56)
	to live on alms except for the colleges (557–63)
	gratuity (564–69) (Matt. 10:8)
	3. Individual poverty (570–581)
	to own nothing of one's own (570–572)
	poverty of lifestyle (573–81)
	apostolic perspective (57)
I	**Chap. 3: Occupations to be undertaken and avoided (582–94)**
Not in a	1. To hand oneself over: for those spiritual men who run along the road of Christ, no other rule except charity full of discernment. Manifestation of conscience; proper moderation (582–83); sacraments (584); rules of the house (585)
II	2. To be avoided (586–94) because of the precedence to be accorded the work for souls: choir; stable care of souls; secular or legal affairs; any sort of participating in legal trials
	Chap. 4: Help given to dying members of the Society (595–601)
Not in a	Charity and love to the very end
III	**Chap. 5: The Constitutions do not oblige under pain of sin (602):** obedience out of love

CONSTITUTIONS 547
The Oldest Text (1546), the Core of No. 547

Verse

7. They should keep in view God our Creator and Lord, for whom such obedience is practiced, and endeavor to proceed in a spirit of love and not as men troubled by fear.

8. Hence all of us should be eager to miss no point of perfection that we can with God's grace attain in the observance of all the *Constitutions* and of our manner of proceeding in our Lord,

9. by applying all our energies with very special care to the virtue of obedience shown first to the Sovereign Pontiff and then to the superiors of the Society.

10. Consequently, in all things into which obedience can with charity be extended, we should be ready to receive its command, just as if it were coming from Christ our Savior, since we are practicing the obedience [to one] in his place and because of love and reverence for him.

11. Therefore, we should be ready to leave unfinished any letter or anything else of ours which we have begun, and in the Lord to bend our whole mind and energy so that holy obedience, in regard to the execution, the will, and the understanding may always be perfect in every detail,

12. as we perform with great alacrity, spiritual joy, and perseverance whatever has been commanded us, persuading ourselves that everything is just

13. and renouncing with blind obedience any contrary opinion and judgment of our own in all things which the superior commands and in which no species of sin can be judged to be present.

Part VI · · · · · ·

THE PERSONAL LIFE OF THOSE ALREADY ADMITTED AND INCORPORATED INTO THE BODY OF THE SOCIETY

PLACEMENT OF PART VI IN THE CONSTITUTIONS

As already noted in our discussion of Part V, a close connection exists between Parts V and VI, both of which treat of incorporation. The word recurs in the title of both and in the declarations on the Preamble announcing the order of the Constitutions (137). Living in the same intimacy of the covenant with Christ through pronouncing the vows, as described in Part V, clearly alters both the very existence of the companion and his situation in the world. In Part VI this new life is even more firmly and irrevocably based upon the vows. Employing once again the analogy of the Spiritual Exercises, it is fair to say that the vows are to the Constitutions what the Election is to the Exercises. The vows effect a fundamental transition. For the companion, his final vows are his assimilation into Jesus as he freely hands over his very life out of love, making a eucharist of it. The Jesuit thus becomes one with Christ, who lives his paschal mystery, who was handed over freely out of love. The Jesuit is introduced into the mystery of the gratuity of love. Herein lies his life as a formed companion. As Fr. Kolvenbach likes to say, the Eucharist is the new concrete foundation of our life, just as it was in the Third and Fourth Weeks of the Exercises.

In his introduction to Part VI, Fr. Ignatio Iglesias explains this new situation of the companion of Jesus.[1] In writing Part VI, Ignatius envisioned the Jesuit fully formed and incorporated. That does not mean "completely finished." Still, he has reached a certain maturity in Christ, who gives him the grace to "run along the path of Christ our Lord" (582). He has become a man modeled on the mystery of Christ, thereby achieving a true liberty of spirit. After long years of probation and training (819), he has come to the point of freely and decisively dedicating himself to Christ the Lord, no longer with the ebullience of youth, to be sure, but with the maturity of a man now tested and initiated into the gratuity of a love through which he surrenders his life. Fr. Louis Lallemant called this the moment of second conversion. For its part, the Society as a body also commits itself to him by admitting him "more definitively as a member of that very body" (510).

This mutual engagement, this alliance, does not conclude the formation process, however. It is not even a stopping point, let alone an arrival. By living continually attuned to the Holy Spirit and moved by a generosity and "discreet charity," the companion opens himself to hitherto unsuspected vistas that could never be foreseen by laws promulgated in advance. In reality, it is no longer so much a matter of "formation," but rather of "conformation" to Christ, a "conformation" ever more advanced, yet never entirely perfect. "Seized by Christ Jesus" (Phil. 3:12), he pursues his course hoping to be seized still again, always urged on by a generous love that gives all for the salvation of the world. This is the foundation and the mystical origin of our mission (Part VII). Once again is the apostolic goal of the Society set down in the first words of Part VI. It is in order that the companions "may be able to employ themselves more fruitfully according to our Institute in the service of God and the aid of their neighbors" (546) that the five chapters of this Part offer some fundamental criteria that guide their personal lives.

---

[1] See Arzubialde, *Constituciones de la Compañía*, 225.

THE CONTENTS AND PLAN OF PART VI

We are called to read and pray over Part VI of the Constitutions in light of an ongoing conformation to Christ that will never be fully complete. From the very beginning, we emphasized the importance of reading the Constitutions according to the spirit in which Ignatius wrote them. To do this, we must, like Ignatius, be strengthened by the Eucharist and by prayer, as he himself recorded in no. 100 of the *Pilgrim's Testament* and in his *Spiritual Journal,* in which he recorded the movements of his spirit. This will result in a reading that respects the necessary juridical provisions, while being above all a spiritually insightful exercise capable of enriching the mind and nourishing the heart.

It would be interesting to analyze the origin and development of Part VI and to learn how the five chapters were gradually organized and set in place. Such an analysis is found in the book by Dominique Bertrand and in the article by Carlos Soltero that we have already cited.[2] We simply point out that texts *a* and *A* have only three chapters in Part VI, as is reflected in the outline on page 95: chapter 1 on poverty, chapter 3 on obedience, and in between a short chapter entitled "Occupations That the Society Should Avoid." Comparing this outline with that of our text *B* of 1556, we see that the latter contains five chapters, the organization of which reveals once more the global dynamic of the Constitutions. Let us dwell on some of these aspects.

PART VI AND THE DEVELOPMENTAL MOVEMENT OF THE CONSTITUTIONS

Dominique Bertrand analyzes this developmental movement in progress.[3] Parts III and VI mark the beginning and the end of a process. One moves from the soul-body framework in chapters 1 and 2 of Part III to that of the vows in Part VI, that is, from

---

[2] *Un corps,* 107–16; *Incorporation of a Spirit,* 253–84.

[3] *Un Corps,* 85 and ff.

the natural man to the new man. The plan of Part III itself is actually modeled on the simple humanness of the candidate. The point of departure is his human nature with its body-soul structure, not necessarily presupposing a thoroughgoing Aristotelian concept. What we have, in effect, is the person who chooses a path for his soul and must learn how to enflesh it gradually, or "to bring it by degrees into his body," as we observed earlier when analyzing the practical movement of Part III. Starting from where he is as a human being, the novice becomes familiar with "the spirit and the virtues" proper to the new life (243). From there he will learn little by little how to integrate and evangelize even his body (Part III, chap. 2). Mixed in with all this will be a gradual education in the meaning of chastity (250), poverty (254–59, 287) and obedience (284–86), and also the consecration of oneself to God (282–83). The individual gradually discovers himself as he truly is in God's sight; thus the reflecting man will gradually become a spiritual man. This experience of growth is analogous to the journey of Ignatius from Loyola right up to his departure from Manresa for the Holy Land.

The progress from Part III to Part VI is, therefore, that of the spiritual man to the man vowed to God through the Society in the body of the Church. Part VI is entirely grounded in the three vows, which sink root into the three fundamental areas of human existence in the spiritual situation of the new man: relations to possessions, to other human beings, and to oneself. This was already true in the earlier texts, but in text *B* the nourishing influence of the vows extends well beyond the vows themselves: it is one's whole life (chap. 3) until death (chap. 4) that is integrated and transformed according to the Gospels. The life of the vows for Ignatius, far from leading us toward a disembodied life, is a path toward the integration of all reality according to the Gospels. At the same time, it also leads this new spiritual man toward embodiment with all the complexities, tensions, and contradictions that characterize the human condition, as well as those basic areas marked out by our possessions, sexuality, and liberty. The complex dynamic of incorporation through integration is at work as we move and progress from Part III to Part VI, thanks to a developing attention to all aspects of reality, both individual and social. This process of incarnation also continues from one chapter to the next through an ever deeper immersion into the obscurities of the real. Beginning with a mystique of obedience in the spirit of love, Ignatius leads us to the challenge of an exacting poverty (553), coming to grips with the economic realities of the time (chap. 2). He then explains a lifestyle requiring continuous discernment by the companions (chap. 3), extending even as far as their last illness and death and thus yielding the fruit of liberty of the Spirit.

A SURVEY OF PART VI

Chapters 1 and 2: What Pertains to Chastity, Obedience, and Poverty

These chapters concern the principal points to be observed by all the companions in their personal lives, points that "pertain to the vows offered to God our Creator and Lord in accordance with the apostolic letters" (547). By themselves these two chapters on the vows account for two-thirds of the text in Part VI and require special attention, especially during the tertianship. For all practical purposes, the apostolic objective of the Society of Jesus will impart a specific character to the way of living out each of the three vows. Ignatius emphasizes this specific characteristic from the very beginning of this Part by referring to the apostolic letters that constitute, as we know, the very Formula of the Institute. This Formula will inevitably determine the fundamental Jesuit understanding of the vows as they are lived by the companion who, out of selfless love for Christ, is totally dedicated to the salvation of the world. It goes without saying that they must be lived in the economic, social, cultural, and ecclesial context of the times. So we must make use of the Complementary Norms to update our understanding of certain aspects of these two chapters, in order to grasp the meaning and force of the vows in today's world. Therefore, to provide what is necessary for such reflection, we will proceed now to a shorter discussion of the last three chapters of Part VI and then return to a fuller treatment of each of the three vows.

Chapter 3: "Occupations That Those in the Society Should Undertake and Those That They Should Avoid"

We recall first of all that this chapter, with all its positive aspects, appears only in text *B*. Here, we have seen, one can recognize the profound effect on one's entire existence stemming from a life dedicated to Christ through the loving sacrifice of the vows. From the very beginning of the chapter, Ignatius seriously envisions "men who are spiritual and sufficiently advanced that they will run in the path of Christ our Lord" (582).

Regarding this chapter, Fr. Iglesias remarks that Ignatius is much more concerned with the spiritual makeup of the companion fully formed and with the depth of his commitment to the Lord than he is with the spelling-out of precise norms or rules.[4] If Ignatius is content simply to mention certain examples, such as prayer, meditation, study, and penance, he will leave the concrete application to the judicious discernment of the formed Jesuit (582). For while he believes on the one hand that the means which unite the instrument to God are of primary importance and indispensable (812), he also realizes that they are conditioned by circumstances which may vary from one situation to another. He has complete confidence in the companion, whom he supposes is directed by the law of charity that the Holy Spirit writes and imprints in the heart (134). "There will be no other rule to give them save that which discreet charity dictates to them" (582:5). This will show that the formation has borne fruit, having produced a Jesuit, a companion of Jesus, a man who is

- ‣ convinced of the necessity of the means proposed during the formation process described in Parts III and IV;

- ‣ familiar with the discernment process necessary to a judicious selection of those means suited to his individual and particular situation;

- ‣ humble and sensible enough to have recourse—and thus guarding against the ever present possibility of subjectivism—to the objective criteria provided by the Church

---

[4] "Constitutiones para hacer Constitutiones," 231.

(spiritual director, confessor, superior), and to manifestation of conscience concerning his interior life, made to a reliable person who will feel free to give forthright advice, something every Jesuit needs;

▸ accepting "with complete devotion" all that is decided (583), and strengthening and nourishing himself through a regular sacramental life (584).

With regard to all spiritual practices, one and the same apostolic principle always applies: not too much lest one's strength be weakened; not too little lest the spirit grow tepid or cold. In either case, the care of souls that is essential to our Institute would surely suffer (582). The apostolic purpose of the Society provides criteria for choosing rules for the good order of the house and provides the reason for avoiding certain activities: choir (586), the regular care of souls (588), endowed Masses (589), secular businesses (591), trials and legal proceedings (593). In all these cases, however, nos. 587, 590, 592, and 594 of the Declarations permit enough flexibility that one can decide such matters, not by strict application of the norms, but by fostering the spirit found in an election in the third time. Reading chapter 3 at the very core of Part VI makes it abundantly clear that the companion, once incorporated and formed in the likeness of the poor and humble Christ, is expected to live always in a pattern of discernment and election.

Faithful to the developmental dynamic of the Constitutions, the Complementary Norms update these criteria for the spiritual life of the formed Jesuit in accord with today's social, cultural, and ecclesiastical situation (*CN* 223–34). They underscore, among other things, the importance attributed to the communitarian dimension of our spiritual life, a dimension already implicit in the Constitutions, as we will see in Part VIII.

Chapter 4: The Help Given to the Dying Members of the Society

This chapter did not appear in texts *a* or *A*. It was added in text *B* as the major part of chapter 3. In the spiritual thrust of the vows, which conform the whole life of the companion to the Lord Jesus and his totally selfless love, the death of a Jesuit is the ultimate step in a life entirely consecrated and handed over to the divine service and the good of souls. Fr. Simon Decloux states this with elegant restraint: "Each stage in life has its own way of uniting us to the mystery of the Lord. . . . In the final stages, as we pass from speaking to silence and from action to inability to act, our lives are mystically one with the last moments in the life of Jesus."[5]

"To glorify and serve God our Lord and edify our neighbor" (595)—that is the meaning of every Jesuit's life and even more of his death, the final and most important act of his existence. He will strive to achieve this "at least by the example of his patience and fortitude along with his living faith, hope, and love." At the same time, however, Ignatius is deeply aware of the struggle and frailty that accompany this difficult time. Therefore, he strenuously urges the superior and other members of the community to support the brother lovingly who has entered on this passage, not only by providing the consolation of the sacraments but also by their discerning charity in visiting, encouraging, and comforting him and by praying with and for him in whatever way will be helpful (596).

The attitude of generous mutual love that pervades these paragraphs shows, as Fr. Iglesias declares, just how deep is that reciprocal belonging that the companion has, at the time of his entrance, freely accepted by his "deliberate decision in the Lord to live and die in and with this Society of Jesus" (51). Was this not the way Ignatius and the First Companions lived? Were they not truly "friends in the Lord?" Did not St. Francis Xavier say that "the Society of Jesus is a society of love"?

Chapter 5: The Constitutions Do Not Oblige under Pain of Sin

The essential elements of this very brief chapter had been written by Ignatius during the first years of the Society, even before he began to compose the Constitutions systematically. Drawn from an early essay written to clarify his thinking on the question of obedience in the Society, it represents a point of view very dear to Ignatius, who never wanted a penal code of any sort. He chose a regime of desire and of love instead of one

---

[5] In Arzubialde, *Constituciones de la Compañía,* 160–61.

of obligation and fear (602:7). He knew that the way of proceeding which he proposed would be demanding and could not be carried out except under the interior law of love and charity (134).

Let us turn for inspiration once more to the words of Ignatio Iglesias as he concludes his treatment of chapter 5.[6] St. Ignatius, he insists, had hoped that, once formed, the companion would run in the path of the Lord, that he would be careful to keep his freedom entirely functional by continually adjusting his personal decisions to the Lord's loving design for him. Thus could the Jesuit measure his Christian maturity by the way in which he, as an individual, makes use of these specific means that are the "Constitutions, Declarations, and rules of life" (602), and that are a sign of the cooperation which God asks of his creatures (134, 814). If he observes them faithfully and joyfully, he will give evidence of his maturity.

Every Jesuit, but especially those who are formed, can gauge how far he allows himself to be called by God by referring to Part IV of the Constitutions. He can ask himself whether he always feels strongly attracted to a life offered and handed over in a gratuitous love that renders him always more liberated.

WHAT PERTAINS TO THE VOW OF CHASTITY

Placement in the Constitutions

The only sentence in the Constitutions concerning the vow of chastity (547:5) appears for the first time in text *B* (1556). Here is the complete text: "What pertains to the vow of chastity requires no interpretation, since it is evident how carefully it should be preserved, by endeavoring to imitate therein the purity of the angels in cleanness of body and mind." It is all over in four lines, as if it were a self-evident matter on which it was pointless to linger. In fact, Ignatius probably had no intention of discussing it at all, since neither text *a* nor text *A* of 1550 makes the slightest mention of the subject. Very likely he inserted these few lines at the suggestion of the can-

---

[6] "Constitutiones para hacer Constitutiones," 233.

onists, so that all three vows might be treated in Part VI, which deals with religious life.

Why did Ignatius say almost nothing in the Constitutions about chastity? Some have attributed it to naïveté, to lack of practical experience, or to a disembodied idealism. Without presuming to speak for him, perhaps we might try to offer some explanation for his silence.

The Constitutions are written from a developmental perspective: they describe the genesis of the Society as a body growing by means of the admission, formation, and gradual incorporation of each individual companion. But the vow of chastity is not properly a formative or distinctive element of the group; rather it is presupposed as a given on the personal path of each companion. It looks to the individual's intimate personal relationship with God and his personal and private relationships with others. In establishing the Society, just as is the case in joining it, each individual after prayer and consultation with his spiritual director or confessor is presumed to have taken before God the decision for chastity. The Formula of the Institute of 1540 states this explicitly in the very first sentence, and it is only with the Formula of 1550 that the vows of poverty and obedience were added in response to the canonists, who did not concern themselves with the developmental thought processes of Ignatius. According to the account of Laínez, Ignatius himself began his new life of conversion with a vow of chastity taken at the shrine of our Lady of Aranzazu when he took leave of Loyola. And the First Companions pronounced it either at Montmartre in 1534, or at the time of their ordination to the priesthood at Venice in 1537. It antedates even the notion of founding the Society, an idea that did not occur to them prior to the Deliberation of the First Fathers during the Lent of 1538. In the light of his fundamentally developmental principle in composing the Constitutions, it is understandable that Ignatius would simply presuppose and treat this vow as a given, while discussing the foundation of the body of the Society and the life of its members.

Of course, it is also true that the topic was rarely raised in the culture of the time: the Benedictine, Dominican, and Franciscan rules mention it only briefly. In today's culture, with its emphasis on the human sciences and the conscientious convictions they have aroused, a fuller and deeper treatment is obviously necessary; and this need was met by GCs 31 (decree 16) and 34 (decree 8). A résumé of the pertinent decrees is found in the Complementary Norms, nos. 144–48.

The Text of the Constitutions

Ignatius describes the fully formed Jesuit as "a man who will run in the path of Christ our Lord" (582), shaped progressively by his vows in the image of the paschal Christ, who gives his life out of the abundance of his love. This characteristic is central to the life of the formed Jesuit and the key to the comprehension of this Part of the Constitutions and of the Ignatian approach to the vows.

In the light of this gratuity, chastity is a direct witness of this total gift of oneself. It expresses outwardly the love of a man "dead to himself, surrendering his self-love, his will, and his owns interests" (*SpEx* 189), determined to serve God alone (53), and "keeping God our Lord always before his eyes" (547). Thus, identified with "the intention of Christ our Lord" (*SpEx* 135), he can be sent without reservation as the servant and friend of all (*SpEx* 146) to announce the self-effacing love that descends from on high. To live this way is proper to the angel, at once entirely united to God in adoration and praise, and bearing at the same time a message of God's love for every human being. The "angelic purity" of which Ignatius writes is actually at the service of "the love which descends from on high" (672; *SpEx* 237, 338); and the companion is thus committed to a total gift of himself, with the Lord and for him, to every other person.

Ignatius rightly states that one must *strive* to imitate this angelic purity. This simply underlines his realization that it cannot be achieved right away; instead, it involves a certain orientation and an explicit decision to be made, a path and a history to traverse, a task to accomplish, training and maturing to be undergone regarding sexuality and affectivity. Everyone is called upon to take personal responsibility for all this. It is a difficult spiritual struggle. GCs 31 and 34 and the Complementary Norms treat this subject at length. Angelic purity is an expression used by the Fathers of the Church when they speak of the consecrated life. The angel is a being all of whose vital forces are fully focused on God.[7] Thus the *angelic* or religious *life* implies a life in which the affective and sexual forces are all directed toward their unification in God. Far from indicating a disembodied or emasculated angelism, the term carries the meaning of fullness, of the perfection of all the human vital forces. The *vita angelica* witnesses to the life that is new, resurrected, and received in Jesus Christ; it belongs to the eschatological dimension of the Church.

Purity or integrity of body and soul should be understood in the same light. Far from implying the absence or ignoring of sex, it calls for the complete integration of this vital force through the death to self that follows upon renouncing the love of a woman and of the children one might be able to have. Make no mistake. To renounce this love and this power to generate new life is to confront a kind of death. It means that one willingly dies to this noble and beautiful human reality that is conjugal and parental love. Whoever has not experienced in his own flesh something of the pain that this renunciation of a wife and of one's own children entails has not yet come to grips with what it means to live the vow of chastity. It cannot be done without the grace of friendship and intimacy with Christ.

In the cultural context of today to which we have already alluded and in a world that so exudes eroticism, often overwhelmed by sexual license, only a strong spiritual commitment supported by grace can safely set one on this road. Otherwise the journey threatens to end in disaster. For while consecrated chastity is "a precious gift of divine grace,"[8] the reception of this gift requires a spiritual decision, a free and deliberate choice. At various moments in one's life, this gift will entail fierce struggles. At such times it is essential to persevere in prayer that the grace of God already received may penetrate deep into the inmost operations of one's being and perfect them in the gratuity of a dedicated love.

---

[7] See Matt. 18:10: "Their angels in heaven always see the face of my Father in heaven."

[8] *Lumen gentium*, 42.

Implications of the Constitutions

If the Constitutions contain almost nothing explicit about chastity, the alert reader will constantly perceive in the text an implicit affectivity. First of all, an *undercurrent of desire* runs through it, most clearly in the Examen (1–133), where the questions recur in a sort of refrain: "Does he willingly accept?" "Does he have the desire?" or "at least the desire to desire?" We might say that the Constitutions propose a process aimed at kindling the candidate's desire. Once awakened, the desire should gradually embody itself and continue to flesh itself out through the long formation process right up to full incorporation. This preoccupation with integration of the *body*—the individual body and the social body—shows that the body as such is not something to shun but rather to unify and integrate gradually in a paschal pathway. In an analogous situation, St. Ignatius calls on the companion, according to the spiritual progress that he is making, to place himself always at the stage of *"feeling in our Lord"*; he bids him to discern and decide in the light of reason, to be sure, but even more profoundly to be responsive to the Holy Spirit, as encountered deep down through his spiritual affectivity. These powerful themes resonating throughout the Constitutions show that the vital inner movements leading to love and to service have continually been taken into account and implemented. For Ignatius they are the sign that God comes to meet our deepest desire in order to accomplish it by means of a Passover.

We might add that even a cursory reading of the other writings of St. Ignatius, especially the *Pilgrim's Testament*, the *Exercises*, and the Letters, will immediately reveal the importance he attached to desire, to affectivity, and to the body. As to his everyday life, it shows an astonishing delicacy. It would not be hard to gather amazing spiritual gems strewn throughout his life.

CHAPTER 1: WHAT PERTAINS TO OBEDIENCE

Place of Obedience in the Constitutions as a Whole

In accordance with the developmental movement of the Constitutions, Part VI deals with the life of the companion already formed and incorporated through the final vows (Part V). Far from being a conclusion, this covenant entered into through the vows opens a phase during which the Jesuit can become ever more formed into the likeness of Christ, who in the pascal mystery gives his life out of abounding love that lasts to the very end. Thus he accomplishes the will of the Father, the salvation of the world. The obedience of the companion is an outgrowth of the obedience of Jesus (Phil. 2:8). This mystical dimension of obedience is obvious here, especially in no. 547, where, like St. Francis, Ignatius refers to the dead body of Christ. Such an identification with the death of Christ, who thus fulfilled the mission assigned him by the Father for the life of the world, inserts the companion into his own mission in the vineyard of Christ our Lord. This theme will be treated at greater length in Part VII. Like the disciples who received their mission from the risen Christ, the companion of Jesus is ready to be sent on mission by the living Christ, represented by the pope or, in his name, by the superior (615, 618). He pledges this when he agrees to share death with Christ through the vow of obedience. For the Jesuit, therefore, obedience is essentially missionary and apostolic in imitation of Christ, who was sent by the Father. So that we can remain faithful to that point of view, after analyzing chapter 1, dealing the practice of obedience by the formed Jesuit, we must go on to look at the larger picture in order to recognize better how this missionary obedience is operative throughout the Constitutions.

The Practice of Obedience by the Fully Incorporated Jesuit (547–552)

Plan of chapter 1 and the development of no. 547

As already indicated in the outline of this chapter and its placement in Part VI, this chapter first treats obedience as such (547–50) and then obedience in relation to the superior (551–52). In these few paragraphs fraught with considerable spiritual content, Ignatius spells out the essence of Jesuit obedience, that is, its very heart and skeleton. GCs 31 (decree 17) and 32 (decree 11) have detailed the manner in which we are to live in today's culture. The Complementary Norms (149–56) sets down the essentials once again.

The key passage and the core of this chapter is no. 547, which underwent a lengthy period of development. As we mentioned in our discussion of the General Examen, this passage's origin reaches back to the very early years, when Ignatius was looking for the best way to include those who wanted to assist the First Companions. He sought a way to sustain and increase the zeal of these new, quite diverse collaborators. How could he help them live faithfully after "the manner of proceeding" adopted by the First Companions? It was then that he wrote a document that cannot be dated precisely (perhaps 1544, certainly before 1546). This brief statement was later published under the title "Determinatio antiqua," a translation of which appears on page 96.[9] In it he proposed two means. The first reflected the importance he attached to liberty of spirit in giving one's life to God: "That nothing [in the Constitutions] would oblige them under pain of sin." Thus did this text develop into chapter 5 of Part VI (602). And the second means to be employed was "that obedience should be lived in a spirit of love that encompasses everything." And this is the text that became the heart of our no. 547. These two means could appear contradictory, but they were, in fact, reconciled in the spiritual experience and fervor of the First Companions, friends in the Lord whose only desire was to live out this "holy obedience" in every aspect of their lives in a spirit of love without reservation.

This text, dating back to the first years, was adopted by the later editors of the Constitutions in order to show how the companions are invited to live their obedience. But the text also underwent some changes in style, revealing the new image that the Society took on over the next ten years. While the text was in the developmental stages from 1544 to 1546, there were at most some forty companions, of whom only nine were professed. The style of the first statement is quite informal, being written in the first person plural. The very word "we" expresses a close fraternal union: Ignatius includes himself as a brother among brothers. By 1556 the companions number close to a

---

[9] *Monumenta Constitutionum prævia*, vol. 1 of *Sancti Ignatii de Loyola Constitutiones Societatis Iesu*, Monumenta Ignatiana, ser. 3, vol. 63 of Monumenta historica Societatis Iesu (Rome: 1934), 216. Hereafter this volume will be cited as *Monumenta prævia*.

thousand dispersed throughout the world, and the text has shifted from "we" to the more formal "they," as in "they should keep in view . . ." (547). But surprisingly enough, the earlier "we" resurfaces in the very next sentence, as if the scribe were inadvertently transcribing the earlier passage word for word: "Hence all of us should be eager to miss no point . . ." (547:7). This more informal "we" continues up to the end of the earlier text concerning "blind" obedience (547:13). The whole of this text is inserted into the midst of the lengthy no. 547, to which both a new beginning and a new ending, with its image of the dead body and the old man's staff, were added after 1550.

Survey of chapter 1

A reading of no. 547 clearly manifests from the outset what a radical vision of faith and love entails. Here we have a forceful affirmation of the grace that is extended to every fully incorporated companion; here we have the charism that is given us to live out. It is not an ideal that can be realized by our own efforts alone; rather, it is a grace for which we must pray if we are to receive it and find in it our joy, even if it does from time to time bring on a sort of crucifixion. We fall far short of living this grace perfectly, but we always come back to it eventually as to the very essence of our life with the Christ of the paschal mystery. In this too we are pilgrims, like companions given by the Father to Christ carrying the cross.[10]

The following sentences summarize an excellent commentary by Fr. Iglesias on this no. 547.[11] He points out that in no. 547 it is the self-sacrificing love of Christ's obedience that is the inspiration and the pattern of the companion's obedience: "To keep in view God our Creator and Lord," "ready to receive [a] command, as if it were coming from Christ our Savior." For this reason obedience is lived "in a spirit of love and not out of fear." For it is the obedience of Christ that saves (Phil. 2:8), and it is, therefore, conformity to his obedience that is salvific for us. Similarly, when Ignatius insists that obedience "be always and in every detail perfect," he is referring to Jesus, who

---

[10] An allusion to Ignatius's vision at La Storta. See *PilgTest* 96.

[11] See Arzubialde, *Constituciones de la Compañía*, 227.

"always did what was pleasing to the Father" (John 8:20) and gave his life freely (John 10:17–18). "To perform with great alacrity, spiritual joy, and perseverance whatever has been commanded us" (547) constitutes a sign and a proof that the mature Jesuit is risking everything to cast his lot with Christ, who is the obedient Son.

This oblation sensitizes the one who obeys to the slightest sign of God's will manifested by the superior even without an express order (547:6). By such a gift of self, the now incorporated companion lives enveloped within his rightful milieu or atmosphere, the will of the Father, breathed in during the two phases expressed so aptly in the conclusion of some of Ignatius's letters: "That God our Lord, in his infinite goodness, might deign to give us the gift to know his holy will and to accomplish it to the full."

In this light, we note certain points that stand out in this chapter.

▸ The concept of the superior as the mediator taking the place of Christ our Lord is reiterated often in the Constitutions (85, 284, 342, 424, 434, 547, 551, 552, 618, 619, 661, 765). This idea is operative from the very origin of the Society and is written already in the Formula of the Institute (*FI* 6). For interior evidence has convinced Ignatius that the mediation of the superior is firmly rooted in the mystery of Christ always at work even today in the heart of the Church, which is his body on earth. It means that God has given to human beings the task of seeking, finding, and expressing what pleases God in each specific, actual situation. Giving due weight to these mediations demands on the part of the companion a disposition toward conformity that is neither mechanical nor servile, but rather the outcome of an active and thoughtful search, entered upon in such a way that the mediation is freely accepted and understood as a sign that through it the companion "conforms himself with the divine will more than by anything else he could do while following his own will and different judgment" (547:17 and 284). "That obedience is imperfect in which there does not exist, in addition to the execution, also that agreement in willing and judging between him who commands and him who obeys" (550:2).

‣ With respect to *obedience of judgment* (550), GC 31 in its decree 17 (no. 11) provides an excellent description that prevents any misinterpretation. Obedience of judgment does not imply that the subject necessarily agrees entirely with the thinking of the superior or that he consider the decision to be the best for obtaining the desired end. What is important to Ignatius is "to conform [oneself] more completely to the first and supreme rule of all good will and judgment, which is the Eternal Goodness and Wisdom" (284). The superior may indeed be mistaken as to the means best suited to attain the desired end. The companion may very well judge that another means is more appropriate. But if the superior's proposal is not immoral and if the necessary dialogue and representations have taken place, then the companion is asked to believe that God will accomplish what he wishes through this means just as he did through the cross of his Son. Events in the lives of well-known Jesuits like Henri de Lubac and Teihard de Chardin are worth recalling in this connection. And there are so many others, mostly unknown, whose lives have been affected and enhanced by this mystery of obedience. When discussing these situations, people sometimes use the expression *"blind obedience,"* but it is this only in an analogous and partial sense. What we actually have here is a free choice to be blind to the motivations offered by human reason, so that we might concentrate our whole will and energy on the Lord of all (547), who was obedient even to death on the cross. We do not abdicate judgment or responsibility, nor do we cease to think, but we do adhere in faith to what is requested by the superior. Thus we enter into the purifying night of that love based on the fidelity of God to accomplish his work.

‣ Even though St. Ignatius does not speak of them in this chapter, which deals with the heart of obedience, *dialogue* and subsequent *representations* between superior and subject form an essential element in the actual exercise of obedience if we are to discover with greater security the will of God. This is highlighted in several passages in the Constitutions (131, 292, 293, 543, 618), and St. Ignatius refers to it in certain letters and instructions. One of these instructions casts particular illumination on this subject. Entitled "Instruction on How to Conduct a

Dialogue with a Superior" (90–92),[12] it suggests several different points at which one might make a "representation" of what he thinks or feels—the next day, or a few days later, or again after a month, or even later—always maintaining a firm interior readiness to obey. This matter of dialogue together with the apostolic discernment in community is treated with some emphasis in the Complementary Norms (150–153).

▸ When he discusses the appropriate *attitude toward superiors*, Ignatius urges all once again to keep their eyes fixed on the one "for whose sake they obey and whom they obey in all, who is Christ our Lord" (286). This attitude makes obedience an act of interior respect (551), free of all that is servile or smacking of flattery. Such a respect can go hand in hand with a fraternal simplicity and frankness that makes it possible to tell the superior on some occasions what he might not wish to hear. Thus can one come "to love the superior with all one's heart as a true father in Christ" (551). It is important to proceed with such a spirit of charity and love that it will be the companion's desire to be known by his superior and to reveal his conscience to him with full confidence. This openness that "keeps nothing exterior or interior hidden from the superior, desiring him to be informed of everything" reaches fulfillment when it is lived in a mutual giving that serves the apostolate and promotes its fruitfulness. When presenting the Society to the candidate in the Examen (91–92), Ignatius had already stressed the importance of the account of conscience for the Jesuit (91–92). Such a provision obviously supposes that the superior himself will exercise his authority in a spirit of freely offered love, as will be explicitly declared later in Part VIII (667). A dynamic of desire sustained by charity and trust is established and becomes pivotal to the vision of Ignatius for the body of the Society. Guided by this ideal of loving faith, the companion will maintain a desire to be in close contact with his superior (552). Wherever he is sent on mission, aware of the confidence placed in him, he will conscientiously keep the superior informed about his apostolic endeavors. His obedience is not measured by the number of commands he has received, but by his choice to

---

[12] Instruction no. 5400a, which will be found in any collection of Ignatius's letters and instructions.

remain a person sent for the accomplishment of the mission entrusted to him. Recourse to outside influences and exterior aids while eluding the mediation of him who takes the place of God our Lord signifies that he has departed from the gratuity and the confident simplicity of faith. Such behavior is tantamount to a betrayal of the mission, which consists essentially in obedience to the Father.

▸ It happens these days, more often than before, that a companion will sincerely conclude that his conscience prevents him from carrying out an order from the superior. This is sometimes called *conscientious objection*. GCs 31 (d. 17, no. 10) and 32 (d. 11, no. 55) confronted this question, and the Complementary Norms explain the procedures to be followed should need arise (*CN* 154).

The Origin of Obedience for Mission in the Constitutions

The place of obedience in the Constitutions

Having examined the practice of obedience proper to the individual Jesuit, we must now broaden our horizon to understand better how obedience figures in the overall pattern of the Constitutions and of Jesuit life in general. Despite what is often thought, obedience does not occupy the first place. That is reserved for the end and purpose of the Society, which is the service and praise of God attained by helping souls. Operational throughout, this purpose is reiterated at the beginning of each Part of the Constitutions. To be sure, obedience is an indispensable means to achieve this end and therefore a keystone in the structure of the order, so it is also found throughout the Constitutions. Viewed from the now familiar perspective of organic development, obedience recurs at every step along the way. But the approach taken toward it will vary, depending upon whether one is discussing a candidate, or a novice, or a scholastic, or a Jesuit with final vows sent on a mission and thus sharing some responsibility for the group. At each one of these stages, the Jesuit is accompanied by Ignatius shaping the criteria—but not rules to be applied—that can assist in living obedience.

Core of Obedience in the Constitutions

If Ignatian obedience is present throughout the Constitutions, where can we find the nucleus, the heart, of the obedience that is Ignatian? In other words, where in the Constitutions do we find the best expression of this fundamental concept as understood by Ignatius and the First Companions? Is it in the Examen (84–86), or in Part III (284–86), or Part VI (547–52), or, finally, in Part VII? Fr. Dominique Bertrand casts much enlightenment on this question. He has no doubt that Part VII, centering on the dispersal of the companions in the vineyard of Christ our Lord, best explains the fundamental meaning of Ignatian obedience.[13] The following observations owe much to his approach.

It is often said that we find the asceticism of Ignatian obedience in Part III and its more mystical dimension in Part VI. In fact, the most common caricature of a Jesuit portrays someone who is above all obedient, whether the observer regards that as a quality to be praised or blamed. This approach reflects the traditional monastic concept of religious obedience with its emphasis on the abbot, or the Franciscan approach—St. Francis was, after all, the first to refer to the dead body of Christ in connection with obedience. But the clinching argument seems to be the greater frequency with which the word "obedience" is used in Parts III and VI, whereas it hardly appears in Part VII.

We will not, however, discover what is novel in the Ignatian concept of obedience simply by examining texts alone. One must take a different approach and look at the complete history of the order's foundation. In the early developmental stages of the Society, the First Companions lived what is described in chapter 1 of Part VIII: the vow of obedience to the pope with respect to being sent on missions (603, 605). This Ignatian intuition was a logical outgrowth of the Kingdom and the Two Standards. As early as their very first communal decision concerning their future, on the occasion of the vows at Montmartre on August 15, 1534, they took a vow to place themselves at the disposition of the pope to be sent later on

---

[13] *Un Corps*, chap. 3, pp. 129–73.

mission, should they be unable to establish themselves in Jerusalem. Four years later, in November of 1538, they made their offering to the Pope, even before thinking of founding a religious order. In his *Memorial* of 1542, Favre will later write that this offering to the Pope was "a grace worthy of being remembered and in a certain sense the foundation of the Society."[14] Furthermore, in the 1540 version of the founding document, the "Formula of the Institute," the fundamental importance of this vow is clearly stated (*FI* 3). Finally, in 1544, long before the complete version of the Constitutions appeared in 1550, Ignatius wrote a document entitled "Constitutions concerning Missions," in which the vow of obedience to the pope concerning the missions is considered "our beginning and our foundation."[15] We have the notes in his *Spiritual Journal,* which dates from the same period; there he describes from day to day how he felt confirmed by the Lord as he treated the question of the missions.[16] The document of 1544 would after certain minor changes become the first chapter of Part VII.

These events and these texts are milestones in the foundation of the Society. They clearly show that the essence of Ignatius's intuition and the force of his act of faith are expressed in the first chapter of Part VII, where he deals with the assignment of the individual on mission at the direction of the pope. This sending occupied the first and foremost place in the minds of the companions, and it ought to remain so for all subsequent Jesuits. That is why nos. 603 and 605 recapitulate this history and turn it into a constitutive text. The founding grace of the Society is recorded in the history of what took place. This historic grace is enshrined in the Constitutions and reveals what is original in Ignatian obedience.

---

[14] *The Spiritual Writings of Pierre Favre: The* Memoriale *and Selected Letters and Instructions,* trans. Edmond C. Murphy, S.J. (St. Louis: Institute of Jesuit Sources, 1996), no. 18 (p. 72).

[15] *Monumenta prævia,* p. 162.

[16] "Journal des motions intérieures," in *Écrits,* trans. with commentary by Maurice Giuliani, S.J., Collection Christus, no. 76 (Desclée de Brouwer, 1991), 360-67. Or see *The Spiritual Journal of St. Ignatius Loyola,* William J. Young, S.J., trans. (Woodstock, 1958), 36–45.

Why did Ignatius and the First Companions conclude that this vow of obedience to the pope was the core of their vocation and of the charism of the Society of Jesus? And how is it that this vow still retains such significance for us, the successors of the First Companions? The answer is that this offering has its roots in the earliest stages of their conversion to Christ and to his evangelical mission, discovered and lived during the Spiritual Exercises. Enlightened by the Kingdom and the Two Standards, the companions spent many hours contemplating Christ, who accomplished the mission he had received from the Father by gathering together the children of God however scattered they were, and calling them to accompany him and suffer with him and thus become his companions. In response they offered themselves to him without reservation, their only desire being to reenact in their own lives and in history what they had contemplated. But how was Christ to send them in their own time to carry on with him the universal mission that he had received from the Father? Ignatius himself recalls how it happened. In their strong desire the companions "did not know into which regions they were to go . . . to avoid erring in the path of the Lord" (605). For this reason they sensed the need for an "authorized other," as Fr. Bertrand put it, to extricate themselves from their indecision and help them realize their desire. This "authorized other" would have to be someone suitable who could credibly and validly represent Christ, render him present. In their eyes, the Vicar of Christ, the Supreme Pontiff, was the obvious choice. To him, therefore, they offered themselves and made their vow of obedience with regard to the missions.

During the lifetime of Ignatius, such a vow required an astonishingly vigorous act of faith, since the reputation of the papacy was then more than shocking, and that for very good reasons. The genius of Ignatius and the First Companions was to choose the pope "in order the better to succeed." The pope, universal Vicar of Christ, was the one who could best help them realize the aim of the Society: the greater service and glory of God and the more universal salvation of souls. Therefore, they would promise obedience to him with respect to their missions. A missionary obedience—that is the salient and original characteristic of Ignatian obedience, rooted in a profound contemplation of the mystery of faith. This obedience is essentially a means, "a venture," as Fr. Bertrand likes to say—and a grace—to succeed better at helping souls. That is because it is the best way to remain united to the One who is the source of the mission, namely, Christ, who is sent from the Father. Thus the Jesuit defines himself as one who is sent. This it is that frees him from illusion and incertitude and leads to great freedom of spirit. The more we are in contact with the world and immersed in the realities of life, the more this "venture" of obedience guarantees that we are, in fact, led by the Holy Spirit, as the Formula of 1550 puts it (*FI* 3).

It takes a long preparation, however, to realize fully that this missionary obedience really is a venture and a grace. The requisite docility and flexibility can only be acquired through sustained practice of the virtue of obedience. It is at this level of preparation that St. Ignatius fully integrates the ascetical and mystical tradition of obedience. This will lay the groundwork necessary to live out the grace and the opportunity of missionary obedience.

Preparation for missionary obedience

Ignatius and the First Companions quickly came to understand how difficult and demanding was the road opened up by the vow of obedience to the pope. Already in the first Formula of the Institute of 1540, they stressed "the burden of this vocation" and how important it was that "the Holy Spirit who moves them is offering them so much grace that with his aid they have hope of bearing the weight" (*FI* 4). And finally they return to the same theme: "[T]he path has many and great difficulties connected with it," and "no one should be received into this Society who has not been carefully tested" (*FI* 9). Throughout his period as general, Ignatius will come back to the subject of obedience; still extant are at least five lengthy letters of his devoted to obedience in response to certain crises as they arose. Experience taught him to insist in the Constitutions on the exercise of obedience as a necessary preparation for being sent on mission. The Examen and the first six Parts aim at promoting this exercise. It is only in Part VII that missionary obedience emerges as a signal grace and as an apostolic opportunity. The proportion—one out of seven—is by itself instructive: It takes long practice to succeed.

How is this exercise put into practice from the Examen through Part VI? In the first place, there are *constants* that appear at every stage. The superior is always a factor. This word is used 348 times in the Constitutions. Obedience is always seen in relation to this "other" who is commissioned for it and who represents Christ. How much more effective this is than a written rule! Both the dialogue between them and the manifestation of conscience render the relationship of the subject to the superior especially privileged. Moreover, each superior right up to the general obeys, and the general himself is the first subject in the Society.[17] In the second place, there is clearly an evolution in the practice of obedience and in the relationship to the superior depending on the stage of formation. It is worth the trouble to read one after the other the following passages, noting the progression: General Examen, 84–86; Constitutions, Part III, 284–86; Part IV, 424; Part VI, 547–52. From the almost abrupt firmness of the Examen, forthrightly confronting the candidate with the vision of faith (84–86), we advance toward the more ascetical practices presented to the novice. The obedience of judgment is treated as an exercise of abnegation (284–86). As for the scholastics, Ignatius hopes that they will reach a certain stability and maturity in their exercise of the virtue of obedience (424). For the Jesuit fully formed and incorporated, the accent falls on the spirit of love and on the mystical dimension of an obedience lived in union with Christ, who gives his life out of a freely bestowed love. Obedience of judgment is considered the highest fulfillment of this virtue (547–52). The Jesuit will be ready to live the missionary obedience that dispatches us everywhere in the vineyard of Christ our Lord (Part VII) when to the greatest extent possible he will be attuned to the obedience proper to a companion fully incorporated into the group (Part VI).

We will be better able to analyze the meaning of the vow of obedience to the pope along with the basic concept of missionary obedience after we have begun our spiritually enlightened reading of Part VII in the following chapter.

---

[17] See chap. 4 of Part X.

Fr. Bertrand continues his examination of Ignatian obedience beyond Part VII. For, as he writes, the practice of obedience, begun during the experiences (84–85) and pursued at every stage of formation and incorporation, does not end with one's assignment to an apostolate. Obedience will come up again in subsequent parts of the Constitutions. In Part VIII, which deals with union, it will appear as a unifying and cohesive force, an obedience through consensus, whereas in Part IX, obedience reaches its fulfillment in its provision for the common, universal good. It is an obedience of enlightened participation for the advancement of the body of the Society.

CHAPTER 2: WHAT PERTAINS TO POVERTY AND ITS CONSEQUENCES

Introduction

"They should remember that they ought to give gratuitously what they have gratuitously received" (565). This brief sentence expresses the fundamental principle that explains all the orientations and prescriptions through which Ignatius unfolds before the formed Jesuit a panorama of the evangelical and missionary poverty to which he is summoned.[18] Through the vow of poverty (see Part V), the companion is conformed to the Christ of the paschal mystery, who received his own human life as a free gift from the Father and offered it up freely and entirely. The Jesuit is invited to join Christ in the same spirit of freely receiving and giving. As always in the Constitutions, these texts are the result of prayerful discernment by Ignatius and the First Companions while reflecting on their experience. We shall begin by briefly reviewing their story, in order to cast light on the text of Part VI (553–81). Finally, we will describe how the general congregations and the Complementary Norms have applied these texts to the situation today.

---

[18] I. Iglesias, "Sexta Parte, Introduccion" in Arzubialde, *Constituciones de la Compañía*, 229; also see S. Rendina, "La Pauvreté de la Compagnie, *CIS*, no. 3 (1993): 55–74.

Stages in the Life of Evangelical Poverty As Lived by Ignatius and the First Companions

Beginning with his conversion, Ignatius's attitude toward money and evangelical poverty went through four stages, which corresponded to the way he gradually adapted to his cultural milieu.[19]

1. *Ignatius the pilgrim convert (1521–1524)*

First of all, there were the first three years of Ignatius the convert and pilgrim. During the long months of convalescence at Loyola, he meditated on the lives of the saints and for hours contemplated the Christ of the Gospels. The decision to change his life, to imitate the saints, to take the Gospels seriously, gained strength within him. He chose to live in total poverty, dressed in sackcloth, begging for necessities from day to day, often enough finding a place to sleep in hospitals among the poor and less fortunate. Reading his description in the *Pilgrim's Testament* is enough to convince us how the course of his life took on ever deeper significance. Beginning as a search after ascetical feats, it quickly matured into a desire to place complete confidence in God alone.[20] When he began to compose the *Spiritual Exercises* during this period, he relied on his own experience to write what might be helpful to others. The great contemplations of the Kingdom, the Standards, and the Third Degree of Humility, along with the colloquies asking to be received under the standard of Christ as he traversed the road of a poor and humble life—all recapitulated the evangelical development that he himself had gone through. The stress on following Christ and imitating him in poverty remains strong throughout the book of the *Exercises* (*SpEx* 91, 98, 114, 116, 146, 147, 167, 189, 281). Ignatius will regard as fundamental that his companions make the Spiritual Exercises and live as far as possible a radical poverty during the "experiences" in the course of formation.

---

[19] See Dominique Bertrand, *La Politique de Saint Ignace de Loyola* (Paris: Cerf, 1985), 216–50.

[20] *PilgTest* 35–36 (pp. 46–48).

2. *Ignatius the student (1524–1538)*

The second period corresponds in the main to the years of study, first in Spain and above all in Paris. Progressively and despite some initial hesitation, as he recounts in *A Pilgrim's Testament,* he came to accept that studies require the engagement of the whole person, and therefore he agreed to temper the radical extremes of his poverty at least enough to receive burses that would enable him to live in a "college" without having to beg from day to day. But he took care to maintain a modest lifestyle based on confidence in God and on sharing the donations he received with others around him. In this way he avoided any undue reliance on money.[21]

3. *Ignatius and the First Companions (1538–1547)*

After studies in Paris, a third period begins. Together with the first companions who have joined him, Ignatius chooses a path as near as possible to the spirit and the letter of the Gospels. At Montmartre on August 15, 1534, they all commit themselves to live as poor priests of Jesus Christ, to preach in poverty. Content to live off the alms freely given after they have performed their apostolic ministries, they would remain close to the poor and would live without any fixed revenues. Often they stayed in hospitals caring for the sick, attending to the dying, and placing a high priority on catechizing children and the young. They also decided to offer themselves to the Pope, the universal Vicar of Christ, to be sent where he decided. They presented their plan of life to him in *Regimini militantis,* the earlier Formula of the Institute that was approved in 1540. Their option for the poor is described in no. 7. Ignatius is unusually poetic in giving witness to their lifestyle: an apostolic and mendicant life, undertaken gladly as a gift and a grace that made them happy. They were satisfied with whatever might be given them out of charity to meet their needs, always being available and free for whatever mission the Pope might entrust to them. This would be their way of life between 1538 and 1547, accepting no fixed revenues either for individuals or for the established communities or "houses." "For we know that

---

[21] See, for example, ibid., 74, 76, 79.

our Lord Jesus Christ will supply to his servants who are seeking only the kingdom of God whatever is necessary for food and clothing" (*FI* 7). In 1541, however, the First Companions suggested that an exception should be made for the sacristies of the churches. But in 1544, after a lengthy and profoundly prayerful discernment, Ignatius finally reached a decision not to make even this exception. His *Spiritual Journal* contains the record of this lengthy process.[22] The reasons he gives for choosing total poverty are based on the Gospels.[23] It is worthwhile to read this account and follow the evolution of his prayer during these forty days of discernment.[24] Fr. Giuliani has written a valuable commentary on this episode, forcefully showing how much this option in favor of poverty owes to the mystical experience of the freely shared love of the Trinity.[25]

On the basis of their own experience during the years of study in Paris, the companions decided to permit the young religious in formation and studies to have fixed revenues (*FI* 8). At first these houses were simply residences or "convictus," as we noted in Part IV. The Society did not conduct classes and the Jesuit students, accordingly, followed courses offered in the already established universities.

4. Ignatius and his companions after 1547

In 1547 we enter into a fourth period, characterized by an increasingly active involvement of the Society in educational pursuits. First of all, by offering classes in their own colleges, the Jesuits themselves began to take charge of training their recruits. Secondly, they also began to admit non-Jesuits into these early colleges, and this group grew rapidly, even becoming a majority in many cases. Hence, the colleges gradually assumed responsibility not only for the intellectual formation of

---

[22] *Écrits*, 313-58; or *SpirJour* nos. 1–40 (pp. 1–34).

[23] See, for example, the "Election of St. Ignatius with Regard to Poverty," in *SpirJour*, p. 60.

[24] See n. 22 above.

[25] Ignatius of Loyola, *Journal spirituel*, trans. with commentary by Maurice Giuliani, S.J., Collection Christus, no. 1 (Paris: Desclée De Brouwer, 1959).

the Jesuit students but for the welfare of the externs as well, looking to their "improvement in learning and in living" (440). This second type of commitment gave an apostolic and missionary dimension to the colleges, and these institutions quickly spread throughout Europe at the behest of bishops, princes, and municipalities. At the same time, this development created a desperate need for the funds necessary to establish and operate these enterprises. Having to deal with others, in person or by correspondence, caused Ignatius to become to some extent a businessman. He dealt with merchants, bankers, and financial networks. Managing and increasing the revenues of the colleges became a constant preoccupation for him. What was to become of the absolute poverty and the primitive simplicity that the companions had experienced and to which they were so deeply attached? Must one conclude that there was a discontinuity or break with the preceding period?

Despite appearances, it is certain that this was not the case. We have ample proof. It was at this very juncture that Ignatius addressed to the scholastics in Padua his most beautiful letter urging love of poverty (April 7, 1547). In 1550 the Pope confirmed the Institute as it had been since 1540 *(FI: Exposcit debitum);* and in no. 1 of this document Ignatius emphasized again the connection to be maintained between preaching the word and the poor, which entailed solidarity with them. The apostolic purpose of the Society continues to be the very reason for its existence. To found a college, or rather "to send a college," as he would say, was never an end in itself for Ignatius. It was a means through which he could better relate to his contemporaries for the good of souls. Moreover, the Jesuits living in a college normally ventured out throughout the city. They visited prisoners and the sick in hospitals, they taught catechism and gave the Exercises, heard confessions, came to the aid of the homeless and victims of disaster. Until he died, Ignatius himself never left off exercising these ministries when he could. Of course, it will be necessary to clearly articulate these college as a means, just as it had been important to ensure their appropriate cultural integration, as was done in Part IV. As to poverty, the fixed revenues would be used only for the colleges, which were the "apostolic institutions" at that time, and never on behalf of the Jesuit houses.

We can conclude from our consideration of these four periods in the life of Ignatius that amid quite varied socioeconomic and apostolic circumstances, he was always careful to preserve three essential elements of poverty. The first was to give priority to dependence on God and confidence in him alone (no possessions). Second, the word was to be preached without recompense (gratuity of ministries). Third, it was important to live in close contact and solidarity with the little ones, the poor, and those stricken by the misfortunes of life.

For Ignatius and his companions, the life of evangelical poverty clearly involved much more than the "observance of prescriptions," though this was certainly necessary. They were bent on being and living in accordance with evangelical norms freely chosen. Ignatius pointed to a path illumined by the superabundant love of God and his gifts, a love proposed by Jesus himself, through his own life endlessly received from the Father and handed over in freely given love (Matt. 10:8). The logic of the Contemplation for Obtaining Love dictated that the recognition of a gift freely received arouses gratitude, which in turn issues in a concomitant generosity (*SpEx* 233). One's whole life is thus immersed in the dynamic of a love that descends from above so that it can return to the Father by being freely shared with God's poor and with all people. This gratuity received and shared suffuses all the vicissitudes undergone by Ignatius and the First Companions in their life of poverty. Likewise, it explains the texts in the Constitutions (Part VI, chap. 2) as well as the corresponding Complementary Norms (157–222).

The Implementation of This Poverty in the Constitutions (Part VI, Chapter 2)

This mystique of apostolic gratuity of ministries that captivated Ignatius and the First Companions would have to find expression in the economic realities of life in order to avoid remaining just beautiful emotions or an ideology. The Constitutions meet this requirement in chapter 2 of Part VI. But this chapter cannot really be understood apart from the experience of the First Companions that we have already sketched in general terms. The plan of the chapter is quite simple. After an introduction that stresses the high stakes (553–54), Ignatius gives some directions first concerning community life (545–69) and then the life of the individual (570–581). This plan is included in some detail as part of the larger structural outline of Part VI found on p 95. We will simply mention some of the more important points.

Introduction: What's at stake; a special vow (553–554)

From the outset, Ignatius is conscious of having broached a subject that is both important and delicate, where it is so tempting to show originality and a willingness to compromise, thereby stretching and rendering both poverty and the gratuity of ministries more amenable. He is determined instead to uphold the strictest standards (565, 572). It will be necessary, though, to pray for the grace "to love poverty as a mother" (287). Thus did Ignatius experience it in his life's pilgrimage, like a mother's invitation to risk trusting in the Father; he exhorted the novices along these lines (287). Poverty must also be like a barbican that is not to be modified except to reinforce it, make it stricter, always taking into account the circumstances (553). He does not state explicitly what these circumstances might be, but he is probably referring to cultural as well as socioeconomic realities. These are the circumstances that have led recent general congregations to issue guidelines and interpretations applicable today, now included among the Complementary Norms. In order to strengthen this firm wall of poverty, he asked the professed companions to offer a special vow to the Lord not to change poverty except to make it stricter (554). This is a very Ignatian way of proceeding: If a thing is really difficult, Ignatius asks us to offer it to God by way of a vow, so that the Lord himself will protect us and realize in and through us what we could never realize by ourselves if left to our own devices. Far from being an edifying prohibition, this vow simply places the companions once more in a dynamic theological relationship of complete confidence in God. Ignatius will nonetheless take steps to assist them to avoid ambition.

The apostolic poverty of the communities (555–569)

Three elements are specified with respect to the poverty of the Society's houses (commonly called professed houses). First of all, they could have no *fixed* [that is, regularly funded] *revenue* (555–56). Ignatius states his reason forcefully: "The Society, relying on God our Lord whom it serves with the aid of his grace, should trust that without its having fixed revenue he will cause everything to be provided." It is obvious that this daring stance was inspired by the evangelic experience of Ignatius the pilgrim and of his first companions. As a result, *the houses would live on alms* and would not own property except for "what is necessary or highly expedient for the members' habitation or use" (557–63). As to the colleges, this question has already arisen in Part VI, chapter 2. We have seen that they were permitted to rely on stable revenues, so that the students could concentrate entirely on their studies. Finally, the companions will take every care to safeguard the *gratuity of apostolic works* (564–69). Our earlier historical and spiritual overview will help us understand how fundamental this matter was in the eyes of Ignatius. It took considerable courage during a period when the whole Church was ravaged by entirely contrary practices. The abuses were one factor that unleashed the Protestant Reformation. This was not, however, the principal concern of Ignatius. His sole desire was to follow Christ and the Gospels, to carry into practice his words. It was not only a matter of giving without recompense. Total gratuity is possible only if one has received gratuitously. Looked at in this way, announcing the word of God, imparted freely by him to us, cannot be regarded in the same economic light as ordinary labor. We are not dealing here with something that can be bought or sold. This is a work of superabundant love, with its origin in the mystery of the Trinity. It involves a life of some insecurity without guaranteed support and is also a life of complete confidence in God alone.

The apostolic poverty of the individual

Here there are two issues. The first is that no individual may possess anything as his own (570–72), and the second offers several observations concerning the proper use and disposition of temporal goods (573–81). There is nothing legalistic in these regulations, which may sometimes seem a bit detailed; but a number of clear criteria are found here that turn these paragraphs into evangelical guidelines. Especially in nos. 577 and 580, we encounter the realism and flexibility of Ignatius, who always provides principles to guide the discernment process. Decisions concerning clothing, food, sleep, and other adjuncts of daily life involve many variables that Ignatius leaves to the good judgment of the individual, always assuming an awareness of one's situation as a companion of the poor and humble Jesus. This is what the Complementary Norms spell out for our own times (*CN* 176–79).

Updating the Original Documents

The course of world history has radically changed since the sixteenth century, as have the socioeconomic and cultural situations. Evidently, the apostolate of the Church has not escaped from these changes; such far-reaching transformations could hardly have failed to affect the Society as well. As regards poverty, a glance at history will demonstrate that the Society has been hard pressed to interpret the directives of St. Ignatius while remaining faithful to them. A brief review of all the general congregations held during those four centuries shows that the greatest number of decrees have concerned questions of poverty. The more recent congregations, especially the Thirty-first and Thirty-second, have directly confronted the delicate and difficult problems that arise when we implement the Ignatian spirit of gratuity and poverty in today's world. And they had the courage to seek and to propose global solutions. The essence of this updating is summarized in the Complementary Norms (*CN* 157–222).

Two fundamental questions have been clarified. First of all, admitting that it is no longer possible today to depend on alms as the source of necessary support for our life and the apostolate, are there other sources of support compatible with the spirit of Ignatius and the Constitutions, and how can they be reconciled with the gratuity of our ministries, so important to the First Companions? The second question concerns the different systems of poverty for the houses as distinguished from the works or apostolic institutions of the Society. During the lifetime of Ignatius, the system set up for the colleges permitted them to receive regular income. But at that time the colleges were virtually our sole "work," or apostolic institution, as we would say today. Furthermore, it had already become necessary during the lifetime of Ignatius to distinguish between the colleges or universities established primarily for the formation of Jesuit students and a growing number of those looking to enroll extern students. We will not treat such specialized questions here. Today the apostolic institutions are numerous and diverse. Besides the colleges and universities, there are many different spiritual, cultural, and social centers, as well as the intellectual apostolates with their publications and reviews; centers for social communications, pastoral institutions and works; and so much else. Could all these institutions be included in the system originally designed for the colleges? The general congregations and the Complementary Norms give an affirmative response to this question. Now is not the time to analyze this matter in detail; for that refer to the Complementary Norms, nos. 196–202. But let us at least suggest some reflections that might facilitate our Spirit-infused reading of the directives.

Regarding the *source of funds necessary for our life and apostolate*, the Complementary Norms began by defining the meaning of the "gratuity of ministries," so fundamental in Ignatius's eyes. They state that preaching the word of God, celebrating the sacraments, and engaging in the other spiritual activities whereby the Society achieves its purpose (*FI* 1) demand absolute gratuity (*CN* 182–83). This absolute gratuity "is to be explained especially from its purpose" (*CN* 181), which is to give oneself generously, without financial or any other self-seeking, to the work at hand and to the persons involved. At the same time, we do not forget that the source of this generous self-giving is not in us. We receive it from God, who first gives himself to us and thus introduces us into this cycle of love both received and shared. We understand its importance from the origin of this gratuity, the superabundant love of God, which is passed from one to another by the generosity of Christians. From there the Norms proceed to spell out the possessions other than alms that the communities are allowed to accept. These include the recompense for work done according to the Institute, honoraria, royalties, and pensions (*CN* 184–87). For in modern societies the concept of alms is no longer recognized in quite the same way as it was in the time of St. Ignatius. Furthermore, money is now circulated differently, in ways that do not necessarily detract from gratuity. Everything will depend on the careful decision to live in true fidelity to the theological gratuity that we profess. Often, as experience will show, even if alms can no longer be the sole source of our support, they still retain all their gospel significance.

In responding to the second question, GC 32 made a fundamental distinction between the *communities* and the *apostolic institutions,* a distinction confirmed by the Complementary Norms, nos. 188–89. The communities are equivalent to what Ignatius called the houses: they are not permitted to possess fixed revenues (*CN* 191). These are described as "those that are derived from movable and immovable property that either belongs to the Society or is invested in foundations in such a way that the Society has a legal claim to it." Salaries, payment for work performed, pensions, and the like are not regarded as fixed revenues and may be a source of material goods necessary for the life of a community. At the same time, a given community may not indefinitely build up these funds, but must redistribute and share on a yearly basis the money and resources left over once its financial obligations have been properly discharged (*CN* 194–95). For their part, the apostolic institutions are all governed by the legislation that Ignatius provided for the colleges and universities. They are permitted to possess income-producing property and the regular revenues necessary for the accomplishment of their mission (*CN* 199–203). This separation between the economy of the community and that of the apostolic work is not simply a matter of separate administrations or separate financial records. Certainly, it should facilitate a clearer understanding of the financial situation. But it will also help the community avoid identifying itself with the work while promoting an evangelical simplicity committed to solidarity with God's poor and a fraternal sharing with them.[26]

These are in broad outline the norms that update "our way of proceeding" with respect to poverty. Nevertheless, it is

---

[26] GC 34, d. 9, nos. 286 and 290 (pp. 136 f. and 138).

obvious that the best norms will never be efficacious if they do not arouse the spirit to desire a life of evangelical poverty like that of the First Companions. Among these norms there is one that reflects the desire "to go farther in the Lord" (81). This is no. 180, an exact quotation from GC 32; it invites the provincials to encourage those communities choosing to practice a stricter poverty or to live among the poor.[27] Are we open to this?

In approving the Complementary Norms, GC 34 understood the limitations of even the best norms and the most eloquent exhortations on poverty. In a straightforward, brotherly challenge, it poses the question: Are we truly prepared to put these norms fully into practice through a prophetic witness of poverty and gratuity after the manner of the First Companions of Jesus?[28] The congregation proposed six directives to help us in this matter.[29] In conclusion, it reminds us that these norms will remain sterile unless they aid us to recognize the material poverty of the Jesuit as a true grace that brings peace and joy, and to love it as a mother, as Ignatius summons us to do in the Two Standards (*SpEx* 147) and the Constitutions (287). And the congregation invites us to pray to Christ individually and in community for the grace of poverty and the wisdom to live it as a gift. This will entail an evangelical renewal of our life as companions of Jesus, placed beside him among those with whom he wished to dwell, the poor and the abandoned of this earth.[30]

GC 34 understood the ambiguity of the word "poverty" in the context of our own time. After all, the Society does not exactly have the outward appearance of poverty, considering the many impressive institutions under our auspices. That is why the congregation characterized our voluntary and evangelical poverty as analogical, to distinguish it from that socioeconomic poverty imposed by circumstances and suffered involuntarily.[31]

---

[27] D. 12, nos. 261 and 266.

[28] D. 9, nos. 278–79.

[29] D. 9, nos. 280–90.

[30] GC 34, d. 9, no. 291.

[31] See Decloux, *Voie ignatienne*, 127–32.

PART VII: THE RELATIONS BETWEEN THE NEIGHBOR AND THOSE WHO, ONCE ADMITTED TO THE BODY OF THE SOCIETY, ARE DISPATCHED INTO THE VINEYARD OF CHRIST OUR LORD

Chap. 1: Missions received from the Holy Father (603–17)
1. Meaning of the vow of obedience to the pope (603–5); what is understood by mission?
2. Manner of fulfilling the vow (606–16)

Chap. 2: Missions received from the superior of the Society (618–32)
1. Reasons for this provision (618:2, 619–21)
2. Manner of proceeding for the one sending (618:3, :4; 622–26)
   a. Criteria to follow:
      General criterion: the greater service of God and the more universal welfare of souls (622–26)
      Specific criteria:
      622: choice of places: need, desire, obligation, persons and places giving promise of achieving good sooner, hostility toward the Society in a given place
      623: choice of works: 6 criteria
      624: choice of persons to send: qualities and number
      625: details concerning the assignment
      626: duration of the mission
   b. Steps to follow in utilizing these criteria (618:6)
      1. Intending the greatest divine service and the universal good
      2. Prayer
      3. Consultation
      4. Decision
3. Attitude of the one sent (618:9, 627–28):
   a. Availability (618:9) and
   b. Representation, when appropriate, of interior motions and reasons opposing the order received (627–28)

Chap. 3: Freedom of movement (633–35)
   1. Indifference
   2. Prayer
   3. Consideration of everything
   4. Going where one judges the greatest glory of God to be found

Chap. 4: Ways in which the houses and colleges can help their neighbors (636–54)
   Good example (637), prayer for the Church, friends, benefactors and helpers (638), Masses for founders and benefactors (640)
   Administration of the sacraments: confessions and Communions (642); conducting divine services, sermons, courses (645), in church and in public squares (647); spiritual conversations and Spiritual Exercises (648); corporal works of mercy (650); writing books (653)

Part VII · · · · · ·

THE RELATIONS TO THEIR NEIGHBOR OF THOSE ALREADY INCORPORATED INTO THE SOCIETY WHEN THEY ARE DISPERSED INTO THE VINEYARD OF CHRIST OUR LORD

PLACEMENT OF PART VII IN THE CONSTITUTIONS

I n the developmental process that permeates the text, each Part of the Constitutions marks a step, a precise moment, in the life of the member and reveals at the same time an enduring, permanent characteristic of his existence in the Society. From the General Examen through Part VI, the focus has been on the progress of the young Jesuit along the path of incarnation, or personal integration, exposed to a careful formation that is spiritual (General Examen through Part III), and then intellectual and pastoral as well (Part IV). This integration leads to full incorporation into the Society. The companion progressively comes to terms with reality and thus to acceptance of himself and of his unique though limited place in the Society. Through last vows his incorporation becomes definitive (Part V). His life is conformed to Christ in the paschal mystery (Part VI) and dedicated freely to the work of the Father. In Part VII, the Jesuit, now "fully formed," is sent out into the vineyard of the Lord. He no longer works just for his own improvement, but for the service and praise of God among actual human beings.

Part VII is truly the nucleus of the Constitutions. Everything that goes before, from the General Examen to Part V, is actually a preparation; and what comes after, Parts VIII to X, is in response to it. At the outset of each Part from I to VI (3, 4, 147, 204, 307–8, 516, 547, 603) and at each stage in the process of incorporation, the apostolic purpose of the Society, as treated in Part VII, is held up as the ultimate criterion of discernment. Parts VIII to X are necessary and exist because of this apostolate and in answer to questions that arise from it: How to remain united (Part VIII), how to be governed (Part IX), how to assure the conservation and growth of the group (Part X) despite extensive dispersal throughout the vineyard of the Lord?

THEME OF PART VII

The title of this Part announces its theme in some detail. It concerns the sending of those who have been incorporated and missioned into the world to help souls. The Society of Jesus is not focused on itself. Progress—whether of the individual Jesuit or of the Society that we constitute—does not form the center of gravity in itself. That is to be found in the midst of the world where we work in the vineyard of Christ our Lord. We are made to part from one another, to be sent. We are not Jesuits first of all, and then secondarily are sent out on mission. Apostolic life is not an add-on. On the contrary, being a Jesuit is being on mission, being sent. The true locus of our definitive incorporation is outside ourselves and outside the Society. It looks to the service of the Church and of the world to be saved. What we are (Part VI) finds its meaning outside ourselves, in our apostolic life (Part VII). This Part tells us that we do not belong to ourselves, and the vow of obedience to the pope with regard to missions is the basic proof of this. The pope is not a member of the Society; he is outside it. He it is, though, the Vicar of Christ on earth, who ultimately dispatches us into the vineyard of Christ our Lord, the universal Church *in fieri*.

It is also helpful to remember that when Ignatius speaks of "mission," it is always about being sent with a concrete, clear-cut, and personal assignment. This is what transforms a companion into the envoy of another and forces him out of himself. Today the mission is often understood as the ideal, the project, the objective still to be realized. This could suggest something imaginary or ideological, something that does not get us outside ourselves. Furthermore, vast projects, when they are beset with difficulties and the crushing weight of reality, run the risk of discouraging the one sent. For Ignatius, the mission is the act and the fact of being sent (see, for example, 612) for a specific work. It is the school of realism that assigns each one to a well-defined task in the here and now. My mission does not consist of my own projects and even less of my dreams, but rather of the work that is entrusted to me. My work is the concrete way in which I participate in the mission of the Son sent by the Father for the salvation of the human race. So often these missions unfold quite differently from what we might have expected. As we will see, Part VII does not specify the missions precisely; it concentrates instead on the criteria to aid in discerning the choice of missions, given the circumstances at hand.

More than is the case elsewhere, Ignatius and the First Companions' experiences allow us to understand in depth the book of the *Constitutions*. Thus they represent a written record of the process by which God called these companions—after discernment before the Lord through reflection, prayer, and the Eucharist—to serve and honor him by helping souls. This connection between actual experience, reflected upon during prayer, and the text is vividly apparent here. We begin therefore by reviewing briefly the Ignatian experience of helping souls. Then we will explore the stages in the composition of this part. Finally, we will summarize the whole and emphasize the more important points.[1]

---

[1] For this treatment of Part VII, we are much indebted to the study by

THE ORIGIN AND BASIS OF PART VII: THE IGNATIAN EXPERIENCE OF HELPING SOULS

Part VII realizes the original dream of St. Ignatius, which is "to help souls." This desire was already present at the beginning of his conversion experience as he was still convalescing at Loyola (*PilgTest* 11). But according to Jerónimo Nadal, it was during his Manresa period that a profound change took place in Ignatius.

> It was there at Manresa that our Lord revealed himself to him in the Exercises. It was there that he guided him so that everything would be accomplished for his service and for the salvation of souls. He showed this to him through great devotion especially in two exercises, that of the Kingdom and that of the Standards. Ignatius then understood that this was the purpose of his life to which he was meant to give himself totally, and it is now the purpose of the Society.[2]

We will not review in detail the slow maturation of the Manresa insights through the years of pilgrimage and study that followed for Ignatius. We will simply endeavor to isolate the characteristic dynamism pervading the Kingdom and the Standards, characteristics of the Ignatian way of proceeding for the good of souls. Three of these seem clearly to be fundamental. First of all, the call of Christ addressed to the world and to everyone in it is a *universal call* (*SpEx* 95, 137). Next, there is a *mission to embrace,* and this mission is understood as an act of sending and an act of being sent for the purpose of joining Christ in the work of the Father for the salvation of all (*SpEx* 95, 145, 146). Finally, we find a *process of discernment* in order to discover whether we are accomplishing the work entrusted to Christ by following in the path leading to him and by praying for the grace to be received under his standard (*SpEx* 98, 36–147). These three pivotal insights will always be present and functional in the background of Part VII.

Ignacio Salvat in Arzubialde, *Constituciones de la Compañía,* 247–63.

[2] "P. Hieronymi Nadal Exhortationes in Hispania, 1554," in *Fontes narrativi de S. Ignatio de Loyola et de Societatis Iesu initiis,* vol. 1, ed. Dionysius Fernandez Zapico and Candidus de Dalmases, vol. 55 of Monumenta historica Societatis Iesu (Rome, 1943), 307, no. 6.

When Iñigo will meet the First Companions in Paris, he will ask each of them, one after the other, to make the Exercises. They will enter, each one according to his gifts, into a vision, similar to that of Iñigo, of God's design for the world, and they will nourish the same desires and make the same choices as he did. Studying the deeper significance of obedience in Part VI, we learned how the desire to respond to Christ's call and to collaborate with him in doing the work of the Father for the salvation of the world led the companions in due time to offer themselves to the Pope, the universal Vicar of Christ (*PilgJour* 85). This decision followed on the realization that it would be impossible for them to travel to the Holy Land. By offering themselves to the Pope, they could better "avoid erring in the path of the Lord" (605), because this would make them more confident of really being sent by Christ and of retaining a universal perspective in their desire to work for the good of souls. The results of this pivotal decision are marked by the three characteristics that we have already observed in the key meditations of the Exercises.

STRUCTURE AND TEXTUAL HISTORY OF PART VII

The structural plan of Part VII found on page 134 recapitulates the evolution of the apostolates undertaken by Ignatius and the First Companions, beginning with the offering made to the Pope. Each of the four chapters corresponds to a particular moment in the apostolic development of the Society.

Chapters 1 and 2

The first chapter reflects the completion of their pilgrimage, when the First Companions offered themselves to the Pope in November 1538 to be sent by him on missions. At this point they had not yet decided to form a religious order. Hence, their availability to the Roman Pontiff preceded and is even more fundamental than the explicit foundation of the Society. The first assignments from the Pope sent them to different places, and this gave rise to the discernment of the companions in Lent of 1539. This discernment in turn resulted in the foundation of the body of the Society.[3] When it came time to put down in writing what actually inspired this foundation, they were explicit from the very first sentence that "whoever wished to enter this Society will be asked to take a vow of obedience to the Sovereign Pontiff in person."[4] As we see, the offering to the pope for the missions was to them of primary importance. What is traditionally called the fourth vow was actually the first vow and the one that gave meaning to the very existence of the Society. The First Companions will continue to assert this in their "way of proceeding" and in all the writings that they have handed down to us.

Starting with the 1539 version of the Formula of the Institute, which they decided to present to the Pope for his official approval, they singled out this vow as the first means that they intended to employ in pursuit of the end of the Society (*FI* 3 and 4). In 1542, Favre will write in his *Memoriale* that this oblation to the pope is "in a certain sense, the foundation of the entire Society."[5] The missions designated by the Pope will constitute the essential and unique occupation during the early years of the apostolic life of the companions. At that time the power of the superior general was still very limited. Soon, however, as the demands from bishops and civil authorities multiplied, Ignatius asked the Pope to give him the personal right to send the companions out on mission. This was granted in 1542, but only for Christian countries. It was only in 1548 that the general was authorized to send the companions among "the infidels." In 1544, as the demands continued to grow in number, Ignatius composed a text significantly entitled "Constitutions concerning Missions."[6] The first part of this text contained clearer directives concerning missions from the pope, along with the manner of receiving them and carrying them out; a second part, presented as "Declarations," described and discussed missions originating with the general. These latter

---

[3] "Comment s'est instituée la Compagnie," in *Écrits*, ed. and trans. Maurice Giuliani, S.J., et al., Collection Christus, no. 76 (Paris: Desclée de Brouwer, 1991), 277–81.

[4] Ibid., 283.

[5] *Memorial*, no. 18 (p. 72).

[6] *Monumenta prævia*, 159–64.

missions were designated as subordinate to the former; and on this point Ignatius states quite vigorously that "the promise of obedience to the pope is our principle and our primary foundation." We will return to this important clause during our review of the text. These "Constitutions concerning Missions" will become the essence of the first two chapters of Part VII. The modifications made later in chapter 1 are quite secondary. As to chapter 2, the 1544 text does not yet include the great declarations that form the major part of the chapter (619–28). It was necessary to let experience speak first. By 1547, however, so many companions on mission found themselves confronted with diverse needs and circumstances that Ignatius wrote an instruction laying down the criteria to be used in discerning the choice of ministries. These criteria, aimed at the greater service of God and the aid of the neighbor, were to be the origin of the declarations in Chapter 2.

An important aspect of this 1544 document is that it flowed from the discernment process of which Ignatius leaves us some traces in his *Spiritual Journal*. There we behold a vivid description of the close relationship between the text of the Constitutions and his experience at that time, reflected on and prayed over. Between March 16 and 17 of that year, Ignatius wrote, "I now begin to ready myself to consider for the first time the whole question of missions."[7] A little further on, he notes "to prepare," "to begin," "ended here."[8] This was most likely the time when Ignatius composed the "Constitutions concerning Missions," after having prayed during the preceding weeks.[9] This period would have included both Holy Week and Easter Week, but he took almost no note of those solemn seasons. The paschal mystery of the Lord occurs at the moment when Jesus accomplishes the mission received from the Father and then, after rising from the dead, sends forth his apostles. Into this sacred context, the mission of the Society is definitively inserted.[10]

---

[7] *SpirJour*, before March 17 (p. 36).

[8] Ibid., April 20 and 24, all on p. 42.

[9] Ibid., from March 17 to April 19 (pp. 36–37).

[10] N. Hausman, "Une Lecture du *Journal spirituel*," *CIS*, nos. 63–64 (1990): 38–57, especially 48–52.

In this contemplative and paschal light, moved by loving humility and respect (*SpirJour*, March 30, p. 39), Ignatius of Loyola composed chapters 1 and 2 of Part VII. Thus, we sense how deep-rooted spiritually was the spirit of being sent on mission. The two parts of the "Constitutions concerning Missions" will be included in the first complete version of the Constitutions in 1549, text *a*. At that point, we find the complete texts of chapters 1 and 2 of Part VII. The essence of chapters 3 and 4 is already there as well.

Chapters 3 and 4

Chapter 3 reflects a situation that was fast becoming common: the companions were dispersed at great distances from one another. This was especially significant because of the well-known difficulties of communication at that time. Once he had assigned a mission, Ignatius had complete confidence in those he sent, and he invited them to exercise freedom of initiative. But in order to assist them in making good apostolic choices, he provided a way of proceeding to discern what was best for these missions.

As to chapter 4, the rapid growth in the number of established residences, houses, and colleges accounts for its appearance. During the first years, the companions were continually en route, moving from city to city and country to country. Some called them "knights errant." But soon enough, especially after assuming responsibility for the colleges in 1547, more Jesuits began to have fixed residences, sometimes in the colleges, sometimes in a house in the center of a city, which would be the base from which they fanned out on their apostolic assignments. Chapter 4 furnished directives for apostolic work wherever they were. At this point, it is fair to note a certain development in the concept of mission as understood by Ignatius and the First Companions. At first, the mission consisted of being en route, of going from one place to another for the purpose of preaching in poverty. To reside somewhere was not then envisioned by the term "mission." Just compare, for example, the introductory paragraph to Part VII in text *a* of 1549 with the same paragraph (603) in text *B* of 1556. In the latter text, the companion is always regarded as being on mission (606, 654) whether he is en route (chaps. 1 and 2) or in a stable situation (chap. 4). Bit by bit, the concept simply broadened, mostly because they had taken charge of colleges.

The general plan of Part VII is characterized by an incarnational structure that is quite typical with Ignatius. The first chapter opens upon a vision of the whole world and of our universal availability. In the chapters that follow, especially the fourth, one accepts the need to be immersed and embodied in what is more stable and institutional. At the same time, the universal availability required by the vow of obedience to the pope for the missions must never be forgotten, must always remain primary. It is this availability that accords most exactly with the original vision of the First Companions (605).

SURVEY OF PART VII

Chapter 1: Missions from the Holy Father

We have already, in our treatment of nos. 3–5 of the Formula of the Institute, discussed in some depth the meaning of the vow of obedience to the pope concerning missions. Without repeating this material, let us note some essentials of chapter 1.

▸ First of all, Ignatius begins this chapter with a forthright affirmation that "the missions received from His Holiness [are] the most important" (603:8). For him, the end and purpose of the Society, the service and praise of God through helping souls, is accomplished through missions assigned by the pope, who is recognized as the universal Vicar of Christ. These missions looked always and exclusively to "the progress of souls and the propagation of the faith" (*FI* 3). Thus, they all will have a universal, ecclesial, and sacerdotal dimension, since they will be undertaken as part of Christ's own mission carried on through his body which is the Church. The entire chapter thus emphasizes this original finality of the Society. Completely relevant when read in this light, the chapter is fully applicable to the assignment of every companion today. Whatever my mission, I have received it ultimately from Christ through his vicar on earth. No. 208, which points out that the father general himself is basically at the disposition of the pope, is just one more sign of the particular status of the Society in the Church.

‣ The deeper motivation for the vow is expressed in no. 608. A description in other terms already appeared in the Formula (*Fl* 3). The emphasis is always on the desire for universal availability in the work of Christ, along with an ongoing concern to be directed by the Holy Spirit and thereby prevented from "erring on the path of the Lord." This apostolic universalism is realized through the vow of obedience to the Roman Pontiff with respect to missions.

‣ No. 606 emphasizes the manner in which this vow is to be carried out. "In this matter, the Society has placed its own judgment and will wholly under that of Christ our Lord and his vicar." This sentence is the same as in the text of 1544, but the earlier text added a line that recalled the oblation in the meditation on the Kingdom (*SpEx* 98): "It is our intention, desire, and firm determination in our Lord." The basic motivation of the Exercises thus appears in this text of the Constitutions. This shows how deeply rooted is the fourth vow of the Society. Far from being a simple juridical formula, it really gives witness to the deepest spiritual desire of the companion offering himself in the oblation of the Kingdom.

‣ Nos. 609 and 610 show how Ignatius wished to preserve a vital link between "mission" and evangelical poverty. This is inspired by the image of Christ sending the apostles forth without purse or wallet (Luke 10:4). The same connection is made in the *Spiritual Journal:* its very phraseology reveals the intimate connection between poverty and the missions.[11] It is, moreover, enlightening to observe that Ignatius prayed over the text concerning "missions" when he was about to bring to an end his election regarding the radical poverty of the Society's churches.

‣ No. 612 makes it clear that the mission received is not limited to the act of sending, but also includes the duration and content of the assignment. Ignatius's insistence on fidelity to "the intentions of the holy Father" is an indication of this.

---

[11] Ibid., 48.

Chapter 2: Missions from the Superior of the Society

The chapter begins with an explanation of why Ignatius asked that the superior general be given the authority to send his companions on mission. Clearly, it was easier to approach the superior and provided greater security for those who were sent. They could better understand the nature of their mission and be in contact with the general in case of need. But, lest anyone should forget it, Ignatius concluded this paragraph by stating that "wherever they are, they will always be at the disposition of His Holiness" (618:3).

In the original text of 1544, the section concerning missions received from the general began, as we have seen, with an important affirmation, omitted in text *A,* presumably in order to avoid repetitions. It is worthwhile, however, to cite it here, because it exemplifies the attitude of the First Companions at the time of the Society's foundation:

> At the beginning of our coming together in one body, we made a vow and a promise to God our Lord to obey and to travel to any place where the sovereign vicar of Christ our Lord might send us. . . . This promise is our first principle and foundation. Some years having passed, desiring a more abundant spiritual harvest of souls for the greater glory of God, and with a view to assisting them more readily in several different countries, we have asked that the superior of the Society be authorized to send us.

"Our first principle and primary foundation" is an Ignatian phrase that tells us so much about this vow. In the Exercises, the Principle and Foundation is the point of departure for the transformation of the retreatant's life. Here we are at a critical point in the life of the group of companions choosing to live under the standard of Christ. They have entrusted themselves to the discernment of the Roman Pontiff that he might send them, in accordance with their vocation, anywhere in the world.

During the very first years, the missions from the Holy Father constituted the fundamental and unique goal in the activities of the companions. As long as the Pope alone sent them on mission, it was hardly necessary for them to discern a choice of ministries themselves, but only to clarify it when necessary (608) or seek further information (607, 610, 612), but always with the intention of acting according to the intentions of the Holy Father (613, 615, 616). Once requests and demands multiplied and the Society grew in numbers and once the father general was authorized to assign missions, it became necessary to formulate criteria to aid in the discernment of which missions to accept (618:5).

We have seen that these criteria (621–28) did not appear in the original text of 1544. There was as yet no experience on which to base them. But they emerge clearly in text *a*, and underwent only minor modifications in Text *B*. In point of fact, these criteria are only the implementation of a single universal criterion that the declarations of Part VII expresses thus: "having the greater service of God and the more universal good before one's eyes as the guiding norm" (622:1). The declaration justifies the choice of the more universal good by stating that "[t]he more universal the good is, the more is it divine" (622:8).

It is helpful to put these criteria for discernment together, the better to perceive the extent to which they grow out of this common root (622–23).

> It would appear that in the ample vineyard of the Lord, one ought to select, all other things being equal . . . that part of the vineyard which *has the greater need* . . . where *greater fruit* is likely to be reaped . . . where our *indebtedness is greater* . . . where *the good accomplished will be shared by many others* . . . and where there is an *attitude unfavorable* to the Society. (622, emphases added)

And as to actual ministries,

> works aimed at *spiritual benefits* and also at *corporal benefits* where mercy and charity are exercised . . . likewise, matters *more urgent* . . . or works *more certain or easier* or *more rapid* or of *more universal benefit* or *more lasting* and promising *greater profit* to the neighbor. (623, emphases added)

It is clear that these criteria envision a man who desires "to profit in every way possible"(*SpEx* 20), and who "desires and chooses only that which leads more surely to the end for which we were created" (*SpEx* 23). This is a man who has chosen the "magis" in the service of God and in the spiritual welfare of his neighbor as the principle and foundation of his whole life. He does not forget that the "magis" is always to be viewed in light of the poor and humble Jesus, who works and gives his life out of love to the very end. This is the only way to understand in depth the criteria for apostolic discernment proposed by Ignatius to his companions.

As to the manner in which these criteria should be applied, Ignatius explains this briefly in no. 618:6–7. Here, even more than elsewhere, the superior, aided by his companions, will enter into the task of discernment and election. For his own part, the one who is sent will enter into a dialogue and disclose how he understands and feels about the pertinent issues, the better to live his assignment on mission in the spirit of missionary obedience, which is at the heart of his vocation (618:8–9, and 627).

Chapter 3: A Member's Freely Initiated Movement from One Place to Another

Judged only by its length, chapter 3 with its two brief paragraphs might seem relatively inconsequential. This is far from being the case. What is emphasized as important here is the initiative and the capacity for discernment on the part of the companions dispatched on a given mission. The realities of a life spent on a mission aroused many questions in companions actually on the spot. Here, as we see, Ignatius appeals to their free initiative. This was already true in the case of one mission received from the Holy Father (see 616). The companion does not lose his own personality or the qualities that prompted his superior to choose him for this mission and urge him to do the best he can. But this missionary obedience will, of course, require some initiative on his part. He will ponder these matters through the appropriate process of discernment and election once again set down here: considering all the options, remaining indifferent (*SpEx* 155), and praying (633:4). This short chapter is distinctly relevant to the missions received even today, although in most cases notable geographical distances are not at issue. There are certain frontier situations into which a Jesuit might be sent where such a way of proceeding could well be required.

Chapter 4: Ways in Which the Houses and Colleges Can Help Their Neighbors

The means for helping souls proposed in this chapter are common to the whole Society. Nevertheless, this chapter explains how those sent on mission and residing in a fixed place, either in a house or a college, can exercise their ministries (636, 652). The following ways are mentioned: to be a good example of Christian living, to give edification more by good deeds than by words, to assist by desires in the presence of God our Lord and by prayers for the whole Church, to offer Masses and other kinds of divine services, to administer the sacraments, to hear confessions, to preach the word of God in churches or public places, to make oneself available for spiritual conversation and for giving the Spiritual Exercises. One should also exercise corporal works of mercy, such as visiting the sick, reconciling disputes, helping the poor and those in prison—doing all these things either in person or through others (637–53). All these works, sometimes called *ordinary* or *habitual ministries,* simple as they are, touch the heart of the Society's apostolic project. They are precisely the ministries specified in the Formula of the Institute (*FI* 1, and in even greater detail in its 1550 version). It is as if Ignatius feared that the more eye-catching works might somehow edge out these more simple ministries. But these were, in fact, the activities favored above all by the first Jesuits;[12] furthermore, it is possible to accomplish them one way or another in almost every situation.

UPDATING

In contrast to other Parts of the Constitutions, Part VII contains only a minimum of footnotes that refer to the Complementary Norms. Isn't that because Ignatius refrained from specifying in detail which apostolates were to be undertaken, proposing instead a way of proceeding along with certain criteria for discernment that would aid in choosing among various possibilities? For Ignatius "it was not the actual content of the

---

[12] See John W. O'Malley, S.J., *The First Jesuits* (Cambridge: Harvard Univ. Press, 1993), passim.

apostolic work which of itself determined the choices to be made . . . but rather several criteria which remain applicable to this day even if the enterprises envisioned by him have been modified since by historic circumstances."[13] The directives in chapter 4 regarding the assistance of the neighbor in the houses and colleges simply underline the activities to be undertaken to the fullest extent possible no matter what the situation, the locality, or the times.

Throughout its history, the Society of Jesus has continued to examine its choice of ministries. To this GCs 31 and 34 have given forceful witness in our own time. The Complementary Norms summarize the essential directives of these congregations (*CN* 245–310) and thus update the implementation of Part VII in order to meet our present situation. At the same time, the very criteria spelled out in Part VII itself show how the Complementary Norms are to be understood in their turn, depending on the relevant circumstances of time, place, and persons, all in light of the Formula and the Constitutions (*CN* 5, §2).

We will not enter here into a review of the orientations provided by these norms. Given the sometimes disconcerting diversity of ministries in the Society, we leave the last word to Father Decloux:

> If the Society is not defined by a specific work, at the service of this country or that, among this social group or that, it is because the Society is entirely devoted to the service of Christ's priesthood, which is universal and which determines the ministry. From this arises the astonishing variety of apostolic commitments assumed by the Jesuits. It also explains that impressive missionary élan that has so pervaded the long history of the Society of Jesus.[14]

---

[13] Decloux, *Voie ignatienne*, 97–98.

[14] Ibid., 102. For more on this subject, see Jesus Corella, "La Genèse de l'idée de mission chez Ignace de Loyola: De l'appel à aider les âmes à la rédaction des *Constitutions*," in *CIS*, no. 72 (1933, 1), 9–26; E. Royon, "Être mis, par le Père, avec le Christ évangélisateur," in *CIS*, no. 86 (1997, 3), 60–80.

PART VIII: AIDS TO UNION OF THE MEMBERS WITH THEIR HEAD AND WITH THOSE WHO ARE DISPERSED

Chap. 1: Aids toward the union of hearts (658–76)

    Introduction: Geographic (655) and sociocultural (658) dispersal

    1. From the point of view of members (657–65):

        careful choice of them (657)

        the bond of obedience (659)

            NB. The collateral (661)

        subsidiarity (662)

        removal of dissidents (664)

    2. From the point of view of superiors (666–70):

        qualities

        delegation (666)

        action based on faith and confidence (667)

        residence (665); places for easy communication

        visits (669–70)

    3. Union with one another (671–76)

        the essential bond: love of God our Lord (671)

        correspondence (673–676)

Chaps. 2 to 7: Union of persons in the congregations (677–718)

    Chap. 2: Occasions for holding a general congregation (677–81)

        NB. The congregation of procurators (679)

    Chap. 3: Those who should assemble (682–86)

    Chap. 4: Who should convoke a congregation (687–89)

    Chap. 5: The place, time , and manner of assembling (690–693)

    Chap. 6: The manner of electing a general (694–710)

        three days of prayer and exchange of information (694)

        interdiction of intrigues (695–96)

        communal inspiration (700)

        election (701–10)

    Chap. 7: The manner of reaching other decisions (711–18)

Part VIII · · · · · ·

HELPS TOWARD UNITING THE DISPERSED MEMBERS WITH THEIR HEAD AND AMONG THEMSELVES

THEME AND PLACEMENT OF PART VIII

Always attentive to our method of examining the developmental structure of the Constitutions, we have followed the companions to the moment of their definitive incorporation (Parts V and VI), then into their apostolic assignment, and finally, as they dispersed throughout the world on mission (Part VII). Having entered with Christ into his Eucharist and paschal mystery (Part V) and having accepted death along with him (Part VI), they have been sent by the risen Lord into his vineyard, following the path of his apostles and disciples (Part VII). At this point, a basic question arises and continues to press for an answer: how to remain united even though we are so widely dispersed? The First Companions put this question to themselves in 1539, just as the Pope to whom they had already offered themselves was sending them to work in different places. The search for an answer to this question led to the foundation of the Society, and some record of this has been preserved for us in the "Deliberation of the First Fathers," describing the meeting that took place during the Lent of 1539.

At the time of his incorporation and assignment on mission, each companion today must face in his own way this question first asked by the First Companions. "I receive a mission that sends me far away. Am I going to choose to remain united with the main body of the Society?" The First Companions responded firmly: "God brought us together and guided us despite all our differences. We cannot disperse what God has assembled." Today every Jesuit is expected to face the same question. As I prepare for final incorporation, how am I going to respond? To say yes is to accept a sense of my own responsibility for the body of the Society. During the period of formation, the Society had concern for me, took care of me, and solicitously saw to my formation. But gradually we find our roles reversed. To accept being incorporated and sent on mission automatically implies that in turn and according to my place, I accept a definite responsibility for the Society. It's not that I am entitled now to use the Society as I please, but rather that it has entrusted to me the task of keeping it faithful to its charism. A new and *permanent characteristic*, a new aspect of my being as a companion has emerged: my own personal responsibility to and for the group as a whole in tandem with my apostolic responsibility.

Rereading the "Deliberation of the First Fathers" reveals more clearly the thread guiding our way through Parts VII, VIII, and IX. These Parts stimulate the companions to relive that deliberation over and over again. Part VII concerns the mission, the division, and the dispersal of the companions; Part VIII, in contrast, shows the way to maintain union within the body of the dispersed Society and calls upon it to let its missionary availability be carried into practice within a specific ecclesial body. Thus it looks finally to the constitution of a new religious order based on the relationship of obedience (Part IX).

The question posed in Part VIII is all the more important because the traditional means then available to religious orders were absent from the Society's Institute: choir, the conventual chapter, stability, common life under the same roof. From the very beginning of this Part, the Constitutions underline how numerous at that time were the forces of dispersion tending toward division and separation (655–56). Today these forces have grown even stronger than they were at the time of Ignatius. The Society is much more related to the world and the members much more deeply inculturated than in the sixteenth century. GC 34 vigorously affirmed this.[1] The dispersal is not only geographic but also sociocultural and ideological. There are members who are spiritual and political, there are theologians and mystics; some members are pastoral or scientific, others progressive or conservative; some are stationary and others are movers. To this must be added the personalized formation and the relationships each one maintains precisely because of the mission he has received. Even if we are united in our hearts, our points of view will differ because of our occupations. Tensions are therefore quite to be expected. One must not pine after an impossible uniformity, nor can one reasonably allow an irresponsible fragmentation to prevail. Rather than being scandalized by such differences—they are signs that the members are alert to many current problems—we are challenged to make the most of them. Like the absence of the traditional means for fostering union, the presence of centrifugal forces just emphasizes the need to discover other ways of preserving our union. This is a question of life and death for the Society; it is an urgent need linked closely to its purpose (655). Because we sense how important our union is if we hope to achieve the end for which we were founded, the inevitable dispersions must stimulate rather than discourage us. From a strictly human perspective, union in the Society might appear impossible. Let us, therefore, form our unity with total confidence in God, for it is above all a gift to be received. Let us adopt the means proposed in Part VIII, means which we must continue to renew in the same spirit, as times and circumstances suggest.

PLAN OF PART VIII AND ITS MEANING

Part VIII with its seven chapters reveals a very simple structure divided into two sections, as the outline on page 150 demonstrates. This structure is announced early on, nonetheless (655). Chapter 1 deals with "means toward the union of

---

[1] D. 1, §8; d. 2, §2.

hearts" in everyday life, and then with "the union of persons in general congregations" (chaps. 2–7). These are two poles fundamental for the life of the Society. Chapter 1 develops the first pole, union of hearts, and proposes means to be taken by the members to promote this (657–65). Given first are means that apply to the members (666–70), next, means to be employed by the general and other superiors (666–70), and finally, means to be employed reciprocally (671–76). Chapters 2 and 7 treat the second pole, to be discussed later, namely, the union of persons in general congregations (677). These are less frequent meetings meant to devise policies that the entire social body should implement in order to manage its affairs. These two poles are profoundly complementary and mutually interdependent. The first pole contributes to the indispensable spirit or soul required to make the union possible and the communion of hearts genuine. The second pole concretizes this spirit and gives it substance. Once again we encounter that same process of incarnation which, as we have observed, so thoroughly permeates Ignatius and his companions' way of proceeding.

It is quite rare for the constitutions of a religious order to gather into a single document the brotherly life, the communion of hearts (chap. 1), and the general government of the organization (chaps. 2–7). It was more often the custom to treat the common life with its spiritual implications separately from the more administrative and impersonal procedures involved in governance, as they used to say. Ignatius would consider it impossible to separate these two poles. It is the vitality of the common life and the union of hearts that supports the government, gives it confidence, and renders it effective. If the body is to be alive, it will require an emotional investment, a warmth at its core, and mutual trust.

It is interesting to compare the texts that discuss union at different stages in the development of the body of the Society and of each companion's incorporation into it. Fr. Dominique Bertrand offers an interesting analysis of this matter.[2] He notes that it was only little by little that union solidified while retaining its flexibility and its capacity to adapt to changing circumstances and to life. In Part III, for example, which speaks of

---

[2] *Un corps*, 198–201.

union, the language is prescriptive and quite unnuanced (273–75); Part VIII, on the other hand, skillfully mingles this with diversity: "the essential bond is love . . . to conform as much as possible. . . . A certain uniformity can be helpful" (671–775).

SURVEY OF PART VIII

Chapter 1: Aids toward the Union of Hearts

Having once established that the Society will require a strong unity among the members and with their head (655), one immediately asks what means are most apt to preserve and increase this union.[3] And here we are not speaking of a union that is merely external, formal, and juridical—even the title makes this clear—but rather a deeper union of minds and hearts that in turn energizes the whole of life. This explains the preliminary remark calling for great care in choosing the members (657–58), and the severity in dealing with those promoting division (664–65), those who are like "a pestilence which can infect it seriously if a remedy is not quickly applied" (664).

As we approach the means proposed in Part VIII to preserve union of hearts, it is helpful to remember that the subject here is above all the entire apostolic community of the Society. The Ignatian vision of community differs from what is espoused by the Benedictines, Dominicans, and others, for whom the community is essentially local. For a Jesuit, his primary community is the universal Society, just as his primary mission field is the whole world. He is expected to be available for any mission anywhere, an ideal enunciated in Part VII. To be sure, this worldwide community is visibly present and concretely experienced in the provinces and in the particular communities. But the universal Ignatian vision still obtains to this day and helps to head off a temptation to provincialism in the Society.

---

[3] What follows owes much to an introduction to Part VIII by Simon Decloux in Arzubialde, *Constituciones de la Compañía*, 277–88.

The means proposed in chapter 1 for preserving union and those that promote the formation of the apostolic community of the Society are basically the following: the relationship of obedience (659–65), the exercise of authority (666–70), the love of Christ (671), mutual intercommunication (673), and a certain uniformity (671:5 and 672). We begin our discussion with what is the most interior and the most decisive, namely, the love of Christ.

The Love of God our Lord

According to Ignatius, this is "the chief bond to cement the union of the members among themselves and with their head" (671). With characteristic realism, in the text of the Constitutions he situates this means after obedience and the exercise of authority, seeing it, as it were, as a theological repetition of what preceded. The union of each member with the goodness of God is the beginning and the source of the union among them. No other source than the divine goodness can result in such a bond, and only love can produce such a union, especially if it is to be the most intense union of minds and hearts. This love of God our Lord is not viewed as the result of purely human effort, but rather as a gift that can only be received (see 132, 812). Compare the thrust of this passage with these words in John's Gospel: "As the Father has loved me, so have I loved you. Remain in my love. . . . This is my commandment: that you love one another" (John 15:9 and 17). The love of God is the source of union transmitted to us by Christ, so that having received it from him we may exercise it among ourselves (671:2). When all, both superiors and other members, are open to the gift of love from on high, then each one's conduct is distinguished by, oriented to, a new level of fraternal relations, on the one hand, and, on the other, freed from attachment to worldly concerns. In this important passage, we observe a movement analogous to that of the Contemplation for Obtaining Love (*SpEx* 231–37).

Obedience and the exercise of authority

Illumined by the love of God our Lord, we are called upon to practice obedience and exercise authority. Chapter 1 pays special attention to these two points. For they are the most critical factors in establishing union within the apostolic community of the Society. The title of Part VIII explicitly declares that the union to be promoted is not only among the members, but also the union of these members with their head. Ignatius pursues this when referring to union with God our Lord in no. 671. In any reflection on union, the head will necessarily occupy a special place. Without the head there is no living, organically functioning body. In each one of its outward forms, the apostolic community of the Society can live the kind of union proper to its level, but this can never be simply a union of members alone. It must always include the union of the members with their head, who at each level gives adhesiveness and direction to the body of the Society.

Given the logic of how the Society operates, it is not astonishing that Ignatius should wish at this point to emphasize the decisive role of obedience and the concomitant exercise of authority. Let us then see in greater detail what proposals are offered, so that obedience and the exercise of authority can function as truly unifying factors. Considering the members of the Society first, union will presuppose that they are schooled and practiced in obedience (659), especially when they are sent out "to labor in the Lord's field." The great temptation at that time is to try to work independently. Ignatius is clearly concerned that the companions help one another in perfecting the virtue of obedience: "[O]ne who has not given much evidence of this virtue ought at least to go in the company of one who has, for a companion more advanced in obedience will help one who is less so" (659). It is at this point that the figure of the "collateral" is introduced (661). The "collateral" was a companion given to the superior as a friend, confidant, consulter, and admonitor to assist him in his charge without, however, formally exercising authority over him. It is worthwhile to read and reflect on this surprising declaration, which reveals such a keen knowledge and understanding of people and the difficulty some may have either in exercising authority well or practicing obedience with peace of soul. It is true that this function quickly disappeared after the death of Ignatius; it seems to have given rise to problems rather than real solutions. But the fact that Ignatius would conceive such a role says much about his view of obedience and the spirit in which he hoped the obedience-authority relationship would be lived. His deepest desire seems to have been that obedience move beyond obligation to friendship. This was the way the First Companions lived among themselves before the actual foundation of the order, when they took turns at being superior. Perhaps it was unrealistic to establish a position such as the collateral. But it is often in the same spirit that Jesuits working together are still encouraged to associate with one another even today.

The observations on obedience found here sound a different tone from those in Part VI, where the mystery of obedience is probed in some considerable depth. Without retracting any of what went before, Part VIII concentrates more on the daily reality, on the real-life situation of each person on this path of obedience, hoping all the while that everyone will live it to the greatest extent possible as a grace and an opportunity according to no. 547 and the spirit of the "collateral."

No. 662 specifies that obedience in the Society is practiced within a well-ordered and carefully structured body. At each level of the organization, a definite responsibility is entrusted to the superior, and it is important to respect this subordination as much as possible without short-circuiting it by going straightaway to the higher authority. Such subordination supposes that the superior at every level has received a mandate giving him the requisite authority. The intention of Ignatius was to give each superior the maximum responsibility at his particular level. For him, as we shall see later, good governance comes alive through the trust reposed in each one according to his mission.

The same subordination—subsidiarity in today's terminology—is evident in the brief outline of descending authority sketched in no. 666. The union proper to an apostolic body like the Society of Jesus requires that the superior general be the source from which emanates the authority of all the other superiors. He is the head from whom descends the stimulus necessary to achieve the end that the Society pursues. This presupposes a very centralized system of authority, as has often been observed. But it is essential to perceive the difference between a bureaucratic centralization and this Ignatian type of centralization. The latter is at the service of a closer union and of the shared apostolate. By making each member responsible for the work at hand, it stimulates and mobilizes at every level the ability not only to carry out but also to initiate and to create something original, reposing in each one the responsibility for his actions. Furthermore, the stimulus provided by the general is meant to be received and entirely lived out in an atmosphere of love, attention, and confidence. This is expressed with delicate consideration in no. 667, written entirely by Ignatius himself, an indication of the importance he set upon exercising authority with Christlike compassion and understanding.

Communication

Having the general reside in Rome most of the time was meant to facilitate communication with everyone, while the provincials were expected to live in their own provinces, where they could best serve as a link between the general and the members. The Constitutions also suggest that the general visit the members (669). For the provincials this is stipulated as essential to their office (670; see also *CN* 391, §3). By far the strongest insistence is placed on writing letters (673–76). The directives are precise, and in some of his letters Ignatius returns again to this important point.[4] Obviously, modern progress in communication has occasioned some updating in this area (*CN* 359–60). We should note, however, that from the very beginning of the Society, Ignatius set great store on everything touching on mutual communication as an aid to union of the group and of hearts.

Uniformity

A careful reading of the passage establishes that the Constitutions are flexible enough to avoid imposing the kind of uniformity that would militate against Ignatius's determination to adapt to circumstances, places, and persons. Today we are much more attuned to the importance of this flexibility, as the

---

[4] Letter 180, written to the whole Society; letter 58 to Favre; and letter 74 to Bobadilla. These letters can be found in any collection of Ignatius's letters.

urgent need for inculturation in the wide variety of cultures prevailing today is more widely recognized. As to doctrine, the Constitutions distinguish between those who have not made their studies and those who have completed them. Ignatius hopes that the latter, out of a desire for a closer union, "will accommodate themselves as far as possible to the doctrine that is more common in the Society" (672).

Chapters 2–7: "The Union of Persons in the General Congregations"

The general congregation as an experience uniting the members with their head and among themselves

Moving from Chapter 1 of Part VIII to the following chapters, we shift from a more spiritual consideration of union to the institutional and juridical elements of the general congregation. For we have seen the determination of Ignatius to maintain the connection between the two poles, which need one another and are mutually dependent. The general congregation is first a lived experience of union—the union of members with head and among themselves—before it is a juridical assembly. Whatever the power and authority of the general congregation—to be sure, it is the ultimate authority in the Society—this is not the perspective from which Ignatius primarily views its nature and function. The very word "congregation," rather than "chapter," reveals the point of view we must take toward it. For Ignatius, calling a general congregation was calling together the entire Society (679, 689); above all, it was an assembly of all the companions, who were usually in dispersion while on mission. It afforded an opportunity for all the Society to come together physically, in person, to live and experience more directly the union stemming from its reality as an ecclesial body. These occasions we know as general congregations. If the general congregations rightly claim to be the highest authority in the Society, it is precisely because they are the Society.

The alternation between dispersal and reunion that is written into the Society's structure shows how the union of this apostolic body is expressed at different levels. The First Companions already experienced this twofold rhythm when they were living in the Venice area before moving to Rome. This rhythm is a fundamental law deeply embedded in the life of every rank in the Society: provincial congregations and assemblies, regular community meetings, and similar gatherings provide opportunities for those who are dispersed but who wish to strengthen their union of hearts through personal presence to one another. That is the way of it: union of hearts on a daily basis; from time to time actual personal union through "congregations."

Chapters 2–7 develop various features of the general congregations, and the outline on page 150 makes it quite clear also. Without going into detail in these matters, which are well elaborated in the "Formula for the General Congregation" (*CN* 331–32), we can center our attention on the following essential points.

The occasional character of general congregations

Ignatius did not allow his attention to be distracted from the primarily apostolic purpose of the Society. Having that in mind, he bestowed an "occasional" character upon the general congregation, not setting down fixed dates for its sessions, thus to the fullest extent possible avoiding any additional burdens or distractions from the apostolic life (677). He specified the two occasions that would require a congregation (677, 680), and no. 679 deals with what would eventually become the congregation of procurators, instituted as such by Francis Borgia.[5]

Those who take part in the general congregation

It is clearly impossible to gather together all the members of the Society. Those who do come together, however, represent the whole Society. Each delegate sent from a province represents not just his own province but the Society as a whole. With that in mind, to send a delegate is an act of confidence that goes beyond the particular concerns or interests of a province or a particular apostolate; it can only survive thanks to a pervasive confidence in one's day-to-day life. This delegation

---

[5] See also GC 34, d. 23, nos. 483–88.

based on confidence is in turn rooted in a strong union of hearts. Here again the two poles reinforce one another.

The spiritual climate of the general congregation

Even though all the companions cannot be present, all will accompany the congregation through prayer. Ignatius placed great emphasis on this, urging all to bring the deliberations of the congregation before God in prayer and in the Eucharist, "so that everything may turn out as well as may be for [God's] greater service, praise, and glory" (693). This is the only occasion on which these three words, which recur constantly throughout the Constitutions, are used together, in order to call to mind the fundamental vision and orientation. A little further on, Ignatius emphasizes again the decisive importance of prayer offered by the members of the congregation as well as by all the Jesuits, that the success of the enterprise at hand may not be regarded simply as a human event. The congregation must be open to the inspiration of the Lord, permitting itself in the final analysis to be guided by him for his greater glory. "The light to perceive what decisions should be taken must come down from the first and supreme Wisdom" (711). This vision of faith is perceptible in the procedures required for elections and for conducting ordinary business; but it is especially visible in the election of a new general.

The election of the superior general

The method proposed by Ignatius in the Constitutions does not correspond to the electoral practices obtaining in ecclesiastical circles in those days. Normally candidates were nominated, their merits were debated, campaigns were eventually undertaken on behalf of one or the other, and finally there was an agreement on the person to be chosen. Nothing like this is found in the Constitutions of St. Ignatius. It provides for four days of prayer, personal reflection, and information gathering (694), with all intrigues strictly prohibited. But this process should not terminate in a decision that every individual has already made in his heart (695–96). "They will seek to be informed by those capable of supplying good information, but make no decision until they have entered and been locked into the place of the election" (694). On the day of the election itself, the Mass of the Holy Spirit will be celebrated. On arrival in the assembly room, the Fathers will recite the "Veni, Creator," hear an exhortation, and continue their personal prayer in order to reach a decision in the presence of their Creator and Lord (698). An entirely original procedure, it is not to be found anywhere else. "But certainly you would not have me believe the election of your general is actually a prayer!" shouted one journalist who simply could not get over it.

As to the procedure for the election strictly speaking, this is regulated by nos. 700 to 709. The first of these paragraphs (700) provides for the possibility of a common inspiration by the Holy Spirit, who impels the electors "to choose someone without waiting for the voting procedure." This would be altogether exceptional; but just mentioning it reminds us once again that in the midst of the juridical provisions required for this moment of intense unity, it is "union with the divine Goodness from whom all love descends" that is held up as the decisive criterion that should govern the most concrete actions and decisions. It has been underlined in chapter 1 as the means most apt to preserve and increase the union of minds and hearts in the Society (671).

No more in Part VIII than in other Parts do the Constitutions treat of community life as such. Nevertheless, numerous observations and remarks deal with it in depth. The recent general congregations have addressed this subject, and the essence of their insights can be found in the Complementary Norms (314–30).[6]

---

[6] On community life in the Society, see GC 31, d. 19; GC 32, d. 11; GC 34, d. 26, nos. 543–45, the letter of Fr. Kolvenbach, "On Community Life" (1998) and his conference "The Role of the Superior in an Ignatian Community," *Vie consacrée*, no. 1 (1989): 7–22. Concerning the significance of the general congregation, see the introductory discourse of Fr. Kolvenbach in the *Thirty-Fourth General Congregation*, 255–65.

Part IX: The Head and the Government dependent upon Him

A. Chaps. 1 to 3: The superior general

Chap. 1: The need of a superior general and his lifelong term (719–22)

to be devoted to the universal good

to be responsible for the entire body

Chap. 2: The qualities of the superior general (733–35)

1. Union with God our Lord and familiarity with him (723)

2. Example of virtue especially charity and humility (725)

free from all [improper] emotions (726)

rectitude and firmness, mingled with kindness and gentleness (727)

magnanimity and fortitude to bear a great deal of the weaknesses of others and undertake great deeds in the service of God (728)

3. Intelligence and good judgment (729)

4. Executive abilities: being vigilant and active, guiding advantageously (730)

5. Appearance and good health (731)

6. External gifts and a good reputation, social skills (733)

Finally: at the very least: goodness and love for the Society, and good judgment (735)

Chap. 3: The superior general's authority and his functions

1. Complete responsibility to build up the Society: delegation, trust (736–38)

2. Responsible for the course of studies and the colleges (739–42)

3. Total control over contracts (743–45)

4. Observance of *Constitutions;* dispensations; experiments (746–48)

5. Full authority over missions (749–53)

6. Gives correction and penances with prudent charity (754)

7. Convokes the general congregation (755)

8. Relations with superiors (756–61)

9. Accepts houses, colleges, universities, but cannot suppress them (763)

10. Knows the consciences of those to whom he entrusts responsibilities (764)

11. Commands everyone by delegating his powers in all that is conducive to the Society's end (765) →

Part IX · · · · · ·

THE SOCIETY'S HEAD AND THE GOVERNMENT
THAT DESCENDS FROM IT

PLACEMENT AND THEME OF PART IX

As we have already observed in our commentary on Part VIII, Parts VIII, IX, and X form an organic whole and cannot easily be treated in isolation from one another. There is a sense in which, through these three Parts, the Society continues unceasingly to relive the crucial questions faced by the First Fathers in the Deliberation of 1539. Should they remain united now that the Pope had sent them on mission to different places? Their unanimous affirmative response occasioned a second question. How could they guarantee unity amid such fragmentation? After lengthy discussions they settled on the necessity of obedience to one of their number. Finally, another question naturally occurred to them: How could they provide for the conservation and growth of the body that they were becoming and whose elements God had drawn together? On the basis of the experiences of the last fifteen years, these three priorities—cohesion, authority, and preservation—would ultimately find their place in the last three Parts of the Constitutions.

The Question of Power and Authority

Having developed the theme of cohesion in Part VIII, we now approach the question of authority and power. It would be too easy simply to turn from this question on the pretext that we are not directly involved and that it is the business of those in charge to attend to these matters. The contrary is true. Every one of us, whatever his role, must be seriously committed to the well-being of the body of which he is a constituent part. Do I take seriously the well-being of the entire group? we must ask. To do this presupposes that we inquire about those to whom we are going to entrust the authority and the power. Who should possess it? If we delegate this power, does it follow that we as individuals have thereby relinquished all responsibility for the common good? If not, then how can we be attentive to it? So we see that giving the authority and power to one person always poses a critical problem for any group. A body remains true to its nature and remains authentic only to the extent that it has a leader. How then are we going to resolve this question and delegate the authority to one of our own? How are we going to strengthen the bond between the community and the one who has the authority? These are questions that seriously preoccupied the First Companions during their deliberation of 1539 (*FI* 4–8).

The Need for Someone Who Would Attend to the Common Good

From the outset, Part IX of the Constitutions affirms the necessity of an authority and defines the role of governance, including its internal dynamic and the role proper to the superior general, who is to be the person responsible for the entire body of the Society and devoted to its universal welfare (719). The First Companions did not consider themselves capable of maintaining as a group the unity of a Society so widely dispersed on mission if they decided to repose authority in the hands of a chapter, as did the Dominicans and the Franciscans. For the good government of the Society, they chose to elect a superior general who would have complete authority "in order to build up the entire body" (736). This superior general is the epitome of the member *totally incorporated* into the Society to the extent that he is virtually identified with the group. His life is entirely consecrated to helping the body flourish. The portrait of the superior general sketched by Ignatius in chapter 2 can help each of us to verify just where he stands in his own incorporation into the Society. On the other hand, acceptance of the general's authority over the group is a *final step in the process of incarnation* by which the individual member is fully assimilated into the body. He renounces the utopian dream of an idyllic community without a superior or of a perfect superior fashioned in his very own image. There will always be something weighty and impenetrable in any authority and power, even one that is evangelical. An authority interiorly and exteriorly open to view cannot exist in the real world. The acceptance of authority in its entirety, with its inevitable human imperfections, is a step taken with the freedom of our last vows. It constitutes, therefore, a *permanent and essential feature* of our Jesuit being and our Jesuit life. It is good to ask ourselves whether, in the depths of our being as companions, we have truly consented to this reality, or whether, in fact, there remains a part of us that is just a trifle adolescent, instinctively resistant to any interference by authority in our lives. This does not suggest, to be sure, that there will not be tensions and conflicts, but they will be evaluated and dealt with after the manner of religious mature in faith. For God, through his Son, has not come to suppress authority and power, but rather to save them. He has taken on a body, along with the impenetrabilities of the flesh that is now his.

THE PLAN OF PART IX AND ITS MEANING

The outline of Part IX on pages 164-65 reveals a striking balance between the broad authority of the general (chaps. 1 to 3) and the authority of the Society over him exercised through his assistants and collaborators (chaps. 4 to 6). Here we find a model of mutual cooperation among those responsible for the general welfare of the Society. In text *A* the principal aides or assistants to the Fr. General were called collaterals, suggesting that they were to collaborate with him somewhat like the collaterals described in no. 661. Moreover, even if the government of the Society can in some sense be called monarchical, it is far from being an absolute monarchy; rather it is a government that is entirely relational. It is a mistake to think that Ignatius was inspired by the monarchies of his time. His whole system of governance was based on the interaction of relationships lived out in confidence. It is a gospel transformation of authority and power that partially relieves them of some of their opaqueness and harshness without resulting in something shapeless or faintly visible. Always exercised within a framework of relationships, the centralized power in the Society can remain truly attuned to the personal. This framework, present in Parts VIII and IX, is composed of four principal poles, each one of them solid and internally consistent:

▸ The living Society as a whole, that is, each and every member, superiors and all others (Part VIII, chap. 1)

▸ The general congregation, which has supreme power (Part VIII, chaps. 2–7)

▸ The superior general (Part IX chaps. 1–3)

▸ The providence of the Society for the general (Part IX, chaps. 4–6)

Each pole is self-contained, enjoying its own identity and stability; this makes possible a relational life that pulsates and is suffused with responsible charity. Each of the four poles has its own importance. Together they show just who we are and how we must avoid thinking of ourselves as living in an absolute monarchy or under a totalitarian power. The four poles are also interdependent and interactive. We have already observed this phenomenon in Part VIII with respect to the first two poles. The entire Society and each of its members (Part VIII, chap. 1) needs the general congregation (Part VIII, chaps. 2–7), which makes the decisions required for the life of the universal body. But the general congregation is ineffective if it does not furnish what is life-giving to the entire group (Part VIII, chap. 1). The general congregation, for its own part, summons the general (Part IX, chaps. 1–3) to take charge and bring about the good government of the Society. To this end, of course, he requires the help of the Society, and he receives this through the assistants the congregation has given him. These assistants represent the authority or providence (the solicitude, as other translations phrase it) of the Society with respect to the general

(Part IX, chaps. 4–6); and this leads us right back full circle to the whole Society (Part VIII, chap. 1).

The four poles continually interact, aiding and receiving aid from one another in trust and confidence. This is the concrete application of the way in which Christ in the meditation on the Two Standards sends his friends to the aid of souls (*SpEx* 146). These relationships become clearer also when we recall the Contemplation for Obtaining Love, especially the second preliminary remark that "love consists in a mutual exchange" (*SpEx* 231). In this way we are called to live within an ongoing mutual exchange of love that is responsible and consents to being organized and structured. Our love is no longer content with pleasant mutual sentiments; these become a love that manifests solidarity and responsibility of one for the others and for the mission, mediated through an authority that is accepted and exercised. That is how Ignatius infuses a unique spirit within the social organism to establish a type of authority and power that does not suppress human relationships but instead favors and continually nurtures them.

This manner of proceeding in the exercise of authority and in the life of obedience clearly presupposes that each companion has made a free personal choice, a spiritual decision to live out the relationship between authority and obedience in the spirit described above. This is a deeply religious spirit grounded in a close union with Christ in the paschal mystery of his death and resurrection and lived out by incorporation through the vows (Part V). The vows initiate us into a new life in the Spirit and its exchange of love "that comes down from God" (671) and infuses a taste for the Gospel into the whole of our lives, which are made up of hierarchically structured relations. Such a manner of proceeding, it is evident, simply cannot be imposed. It calls for volunteers entering upon complete reciprocal confidence and living out the manifestation of conscience so fundamental to the Society (92, 764).

SURVEY OF PART IX

Without providing a running commentary or a textual analysis, we highlight certain points that will help us in our spiritually perceptive reading. Noteworthy at the outset is the title announcing the "government that descends from it." It recalls "the love that descends from the divine Goodness" (671) and "all the gifts that descend from on high" (*SpEx* 237) in the Contemplation for Obtaining Love. For Ignatius everything is understood in the light of grace and God's free gift. One has only to remember the illumination at the river Cardoner (*Pilg-Test* 30) and the manner in which he "made" the Constitutions, as described in his testament (99–100). The governance of the Society is likewise viewed from this perspective, not so much as a chastisement but rather as a grace and a gift from God.

The Superior General (Chapters 1 to 3)

Chapter 1

The task of the superior general as well of as his assistants is to devote themselves to the universal good. We sometimes think of government in terms of coordination, checks and balances. This is not the Ignatian view: the general is responsible for the entire body and should govern it. Furthermore, he is elected for life and Ignatius gives the reasons for this (719–22). Nevertheless, GC 31 judged it necessary to foresee the possibility that the general might resign (*CN* 362, 366). Ignatius himself in fact wished to be relieved of office and had offered his own resignation at the meeting of the principal fathers of the Society in 1550.[1]

Chapter 2: The qualities that the general should possess

The entire chapter deserves careful meditation.[2] Here the ideal of the father general is described by Ignatius, and we are happy to recognize our founder in this description. But, of course, every companion can see this as a description of what he himself is called to be, in accordance with God's grace. Indeed, each of us will recognize how far he is from such an ideal. At the same time, the portrait sketched by Ignatius does reveal what he actually hoped to find in each companion. Most

---

[1] Letter 1554, in any collection of Ignatius's letters.

[2] See the commentary by Fr. S. Decloux in *Voie ignatienne*, 201–6.

important is the Jesuit's spiritual and moral quality that, along with the solicitous care with which he was formed and the clarity of his judgment, will equip him to serve well those to whom he is sent. These very qualities will empower him to guide the apostolic efforts of a group under his charge and to energize a Christian community, leading it faithfully according to the grace received and in union with the whole body of the Society. This description of the superior general will seem more relevant to the life of each companion if read with attention to the last paragraph, which puts everything in a different light and brings it down to earth. "If any of the aforementioned qualities should be wanting, he should at least not lack great goodness and a love for the Society, nor good judgment accompanied by sound learning" (735). For Ignatius, the word "goodness" (*bondad*) carried a depth of meaning and uncommon connotations; he often signed his earlier letters "Iñigo, pobre en bondad," referring to that goodness which descends from the essence of goodness, which is God. This leads us back, of course, to no. 671 and the Contemplation for Obtaining Love (*SpEx* 237).

Chapter 3: The authority of the general and his functions

This chapter, one of the longest in the Constitutions, strikes us with the broad authority it imparts to the general, and is also among the most controversial chapters in the Constitutions, both outside the Society and within it. It has been called "spiritual despotism, unlimited power without boundaries. Such an authority resembles a ferocious beast that, unless it is securely tied down, destroys everything." But the critics do not take into account that from the very first paragraph this authority of the general is given "in order to build up" the Society (736), and text A adds "and not for its destruction," a phrase that was not retained in later editions. The next two chapters, however, are exclusively occupied with the providence, the vigilance, exercised by the Society in regard to the general, exercised in the persons of the four assistants, elected by the general congregation itself. One of the tasks given to the assistants is to impede any action by the general that is harmful or contrary to the well-being of the Society. Moreover, the fullness of the general's authority should not be considered exclusive, as if all power rested in his hands alone. In him authority has its source and thus its plenitude. The authority of the other superiors is communicated through him and derives from him. He delegates it with confidence: first he nominates someone, then bestows the powers that he believes are for the glory of God and the welfare of souls (757, 759). This is a manner of proceeding quite different from what obtains in other religious orders, where local superiors are elected by the community and thereby receive their power.

In chapter 3, which specifies the authority of the superior general and his responsibilities (see the outline on pages 164-65), the whole of the Constitutions seems to pass in review, for the chief duty of the general is to cause the Constitutions to be lived and observed (746–47). Anyone reading this text will exclaim, "What a 'man of affairs' the general has to be!" True, the office itself thrusts him into administrative activities. All one has to do is read through the correspondence of St. Ignatius to be convinced of this; but, of course, the challenge is to manage all these affairs in the spirit of the Gospel and thus "to seek and find God in all things."

The power of the general is also very personal. This is explicitly stated in nos. 736, 747, and 809, but it can be found everywhere, especially in those many exhortations for the general "to decide as he judges good and opportune and in accordance with what he believes to be best in the Lord (739, 740, 744, 746, 747, 749, 753, and so on). He is a man always in a state of discernment and election. At the same time, the emphasis is always firmly placed on *delegation with confidence* (736, 737, 740, 745, 747, 752, and so on). That is actually the secret of his activity: he must with complete confidence delegate much of his authority to others. He continues, however, to be responsible personally for everything and must remain aware of whatever is more important (for example, his manner of proceeding with the provincials, 797). He cannot wash his hands of the powers once he has delegated them, for the source of this authority and power remains with him. The last paragraphs of this chapter (764–65) provide the key to successful governance of this kind: the mutual confidence that grows out of the "openness of conscience" freely accepted and practiced as part of the Jesuit charism beginning with one's entrance into the Society ("Examen" 92). These relationships of confident openness allow superiors to exercise their authority by a generous delegation or communication of power, for the relationships are rooted in a close union with Christ, in whose place superiors act (795). These relationships are also fostered by the dynamism of the Exercises, which culminates in the risen Christ sending the Spirit, and introduces anew into the world that exchange of love and mutual communion described in the Contemplation for Obtaining Love. Thanks to this atmosphere of confidence and complete singleness of purpose, the superior general is able to exercise such power; he is certainly not alone, as the following chapter will more directly confirm.

At this stage in our study of the Constitutions, we realize more clearly the meaning and importance of the account of conscience explained to the candidate applying for admission to the Society (92). Its raison d'être is essentially apostolic and oriented primarily toward the mission, as is mentioned, moreover, in no. 92. To be sure, at the beginning of the religious life it is a spiritual aid, as it is in the great monastic and religious tradition; but gradually and increasingly, as one is incorporated and sent on mission, the account of conscience will be truly spiritual in proportion to its becoming apostolic as well. The two are inseparable, just as the government of the Society is indissolubly spiritual and apostolic.

The Authority or Solicitude of the Society with Respect to the Father General (Chapters 4–6)

After having detailed in the first three chapters all the authority and power of the superior general for the "upbuilding" of the Society, the three following chapters deal with relations between the Society and the general. Here again everything is organized so as to keep the different poles constantly interacting with one another through an interplay of relations maintained in full confidence. This confidence includes also a loving vigilance and a respectful solicitude. These three chapters—4, 5, and 6—make only too obvious that the general is not endowed with absolute power, but is himself surrounded by the loving watchfulness of the Society. The presence of the Society to anything that concerns the father general in no way detracts from the depth or the purifying force or, in the final analysis, from the fruitfulness of his own presence to the Society, as no. 765 bids us desire for him.[3]

Chapter 4: The authority or provident care which the Society should exercise in regard to the superior general

The general himself is subject to supervision! Actually he is the first subject of the Society right down to the details of his daily life (768–70). And Ignatius goes so far as to foresee the very worst scenario (774). The word "providence," added by him to the title to suggest the authority of the Society,[4] is priceless, for it implies that this authority is built upon the loving providence of God. This providence is in real life supplied by the four general assistants elected by the general congregation to watch over father general (767). Ignatius justifies this in a note in his own hand appended to a preparatory version of the Constitutions, and it says much about his understanding of his role and function as superior.

Concerning the providence, the authority, and the vigilance that the Society should have in regard to the general.

The Society or the persons designated by it will in love and charity exercise the providence required for all external matters that are necessary and appropriate for the superior general. Hence they will decide, determine, and provide for his food . . . which is no small spiritual favor for two reasons. First of all, supposing the superior to be the kind we would hope for, his spiritual consolation and contentment would be great if he were free from such concerns about which he would wish and desire simply to obey the Society as holding the place of Christ our Lord. Secondly, the subjects of the Society, learning of this disposition, will have no reason to be disedified, which in turn will promote a closer union of the head with the members.[5]

---

[3] Bertrand, *Un Corps*, 194.

[4] Giuliani, *Écrits*, 587 n.

[5] *Monumenta prævia*, p. 385.

Chapter 5

This is a somber chapter. Ignatius understands human weakness, and must therefore provide for the possibility of malfeasance on the part of the general. At this juncture it is made clear that the provincials are not just "the general's men," as would be the case if the general possessed absolute power. They are responsible for the universal welfare of the Society (778, 782:3) and must shoulder their responsibilities. In this chapter Ignatius specifies the tasks of the four assistants, who personify the authority and solicitude of the whole Society with respect to the general (779–81; CN 363–66). He will return in chapter 6 with other details of their duties. Nos. 783 and 785 reflect that delicacy and respect for individuals, which also characterized the passages in Part II concerned with dismissal from the Society.

Chapter 6: Aids to the superior general for the proper performance of his functions

‣ The outline of Part IX on pages 164-65 above presents the essence of this chapter. The better to understand actual, practical procedures, we must consult the modifications and clarifications detailed in the Complementary Norms (CN 362–86). Nevertheless, the spirit emanating from the original text of the Constitutions remains entirely relevant to this day.

‣ The first paragraph of this chapter (789) along with its declaration (790) is an excellent resume of the general's mandate.

‣ It becomes evident that misconduct and suspicion play no part in the authority of this Society, but rather the desire of the father general to obey in all things the Society, which holds for him the place of Christ our Lord. This interchange between governor and governed is the fruit of obedience. The superior general who exercises full authority within the Society is himself the one whose whole life is obedience to the group.

‣ Through the aides who are furnished to him and by means of the delegation of power that he himself practices, the general will be able to accomplish what is required of him in chapter 3. This is just one more indication that Ignatius holds delegation, communication with trusted advisors, to be the first rule of power. For this reason, solid evidence of reliability must be available through frequent correspondence, meetings, and the like (795, 797).

▸ The essential function of the "collateral" remains operative at all times in the functions assigned to the various aides appointed for the father general. This is especially obvious in the case of the secretary of the Society (800–802). As to the assistants (803–5), we have already noted that they were called "collaterals" in one of the earlier version of the Constitutions, namely, text *A*.

▸ No. 809 is yet another expression of the extent to which the life of the father general must be devoted entirely to obedience serving the universal good of the Society.

▸ As to the final declaration of Part IX (811), why couldn't it be read as a call to every individual companion to let himself be inspired by this portrait of the superior general and thus strive for full incorporation into the Society, each one according to the grace given to him and the circumstances of his life?

Part X: How the Whole Body of the Society Is to Be Preserved and Increased in Its Well-Being

A. Hope in God alone and Search for Means (812–15)

1. The purpose and fundamental means. Since God is the origin of the Society (812), our hope is in him alone; therefore prayers and Masses weekly, monthly, and yearly.

2. The spiritual means: union of the instrument with God (813): to devote themselves to the solid and perfect virtues and to spiritual pursuits, and attach greater importance to these than to learning and other natural and human gifts.

3. The human means: they are integrated into faith (814), which is exercised with confidence in God. Creation assumed by God.

4. The institutional means: rootedness in the "embodied" world (815); college viewed here as a source of vocations.

B. The Internal Life of the Society: Discernment of spiritual means; (repetition of and expansion upon no. 813) (816–22)

1. Poverty safeguarding gratuity (816)

2. Exclusion of ambition, thanks to humility
   a. Promise not to seek dignities (817)
   b. Promise to expose one who seeks dignities
   c. Promise to refuse every dignity except under obedience Each one should desire to serve souls in conformity with our profession of humility and lowliness
   d. Promise to listen to the counsel of the general if one becomes a prelate by virtue of obedience

3. To establish the Society as a body in accordance with the Constitutions
   a. Admission to the profession carefully decided (819)
   b. Importance of the general and of superiors (820)
   c. Concern for unity: bond of will and mutual love
   d. Moderation in labor of both mind and body (822)

C. The Apostolic Life of the Society: Discernment of certain human means (repetition of no. 814) (823–27)

1. Efforts to cultivate goodwill with all (823–24)

2. Moderate use of privileges granted by the Holy See (825)

3. Health care; knowledge of the Constitutions and reading them (826); salubrious location of houses (827)

Part X · · · · · ·

How the Whole Body of the Society Is to Be Preserved and Increased in Its Well-Being

---

Placement and Subject Matter of Part X

The developmental approach that pervades the Constitutions has enabled us to retrace the various steps leading to the assimilation of each individual into the group. It has also helped us understand the process of development of the whole Society and the way it can remain united even though it is dispersed. What does Part X add to this picture, which seemed complete with the conclusion of Part IX?

Part X does not center on a single step, a particular moment, in the gradual process of integration into the group; rather, it takes a look at the totality of the Society's life. Each of the first nine parts deals with the standards and criteria applicable to specific periods in the life of each companion and in that of the Society as a whole. Part X, however, proposes basic criteria and procedures that must be kept in mind at all times and in every circumstance for the welfare of the Society and all of its members. By attending to these points, the Society will always be able to rediscover and reinvent itself anew in the midst of continually shifting historical, social, and cultural circumstances. It will be able to accomplish this with a creative fidelity to its own proper identity as defined in the Formula of the Institute. "To act as our predecessors did, we must act differently from them," said one provincial, P. C. Plaquet. Respect for the perspectives spread before us in Part X and for the principles enunciated there will make us genuinely responsible for the Society, ready always to found it anew without becoming its owners or bending it to our own personal preferences, but acting always in accordance with the charism confided to us.

Part X immediately returns to the overall objective of the Constitutions. Its title almost literally repeats what Ignatius wrote earlier regarding the end of the Society: "The purpose of the Constitutions is to aid the body of the Society as a whole and its individual members toward their preservation and *increase* for the divine glory and the good of the Church" (136:2, emphasis added). Texts *a* and *A* of 1550 begin with these lines. Clearly then, the objective of Part X is closely identified with the general purpose of the Constitutions; thus it expresses what is essential in the Constitutions and imparts living spirit to it. It illuminates the meaning of each of the parts as well as the complete process and supplies the key to an accurate interpretation. Certain commentators actually suggest that the study of the Constitutions should begin with Part X.

Far from being a conclusion, Part X functions more as a beginning and as illumination for the future. In contrast to the preceding parts, the words used in its very title point toward the future. Ignatius did not really lock up the Constitutions or bring them to a rigid conclusion. Rather, he left them open to new life and to the future, providing at the same time such criteria for discernment as might aid in living out that future. A comparison with the Spiritual Exercises is enlightening. The Exercises are not an experience closed in on themselves; rather, they send the exercitant back into the world and into everyday life. That is the meaning of the Fourth Week and especially of the Contemplation for Obtaining Love. The retreatant is drawn outside himself toward the future. That is where God awaits him and where he is called to seek and find God in everything. The same is true of the Constitutions, which is not shut in on itself. By virtue of its apostolic purpose, the Society needs to come out of itself for its own preservation and growth. It must ever remain boldly open to the future if it is to accomplish those missions ultimately entrusted to it by the Vicar of Christ. This is essential to its vitality and progress. That is why the Constitutions finish with Part X, which directs our attention toward the future, toward an ongoing apostolic engagement to work for the good of souls "for the glory of God, and the welfare of the universal Church" (136). Fr. M. Costa calls Part X "a contemplation for obtaining hope."[1] Hope is the fundamental attitude of the apostle working always with an eye to the future.

STRUCTURE OF PART X

Part X consists of only one chapter with thirteen paragraphs and three declarations. Of all the parts of the Constitutions it is the shortest but not the least important—far from it. On first reading , it may seem to be a succession of counsels proposed without much order. But on closer inspection, we can perceive a certain structure (see the structural plan on page 178). Most commentators content themselves with finding two sections in Part X. The first section (812–14) lays down a basic attitude along with the means necessary to sustain it, and the second section (815–27) deals with more particular means and methods for preserving the whole Society in its well-being. This division is based on the verbs used to introduce the paragraphs that develop these different means and methods. In the first three paragraphs that form the first section (812–14), we find verbs expressing obligation: "one must," "it is necessary," and the like. The context has to do with fundamental values. In the second section (815–27), the verbs are less peremptory: "it will be important," or "it will be profitable," or "it will be found helpful." In addition, some more specific criteria and means seem to have been proposed with little apparent order.

Fr. Dominique Bertrand, however, has suggested a somewhat more detailed structure for this second section based on an analysis of the logical connections around its two key pas-

---

[1] Consult the various works by Father M. Costa, S.J., on Part X, as well as his book *Legge religiosa e discernimento spirituale nelle Constituzione della Compagnía di Gesù* (Brescia, 1973). In the following pages we are much indebted to him and to others.

sages, nos. 815 and 822–23, and also on a study of important words: "body" and "spirit," "help" and "to help," "to maintain" and "to conserve." We will not go into great detail regarding this analysis, but the structural outline on page 178 summarizes it and shows, we believe, that this second section is more elaborately organized than it seemed to be at first examination, and also that it brings certain very important points forward and places them in evidence. We limit ourselves to one example, perhaps the most significant. In the preparatory text of the Constitutions drafted by Polanco (*Industriæ* of 1548), no. 815 concerning the colleges was placed after nos. 817–18 concerning ambition. In texts *a* and *A* of 1550, no. 815 is taken out and brought forward to its present location. In addition, text *B* of 1556 has the word "equally" added at the beginning, thus associating no. 815 with the preceding paragraph concerning human means. In view of all these changes, no. 815 was placed in the first section, thus acquiring a considerable importance, the significance of which we will soon see.

An examination of Part X as a whole shows that numerous means and criteria already treated at length in earlier parts of the Constitutions are mentioned briefly here; in fact, the text regularly refers back to the location where they were previously discussed. In this way, most of the key points in the Constitutions are cited once again, and almost every paragraph of this Part X refers back to something treated earlier. The aim here is not so much to recapitulate these issues by way of conclusion but rather to advance them as criteria and means intended to be put into practice in the future.

SURVEY OF PART X: A CONTEMPLATION FOR OBTAINING HOPE

Hope in God Alone and Implementation of Fundamental Means (812–815)

It seems obvious enough that Ignatius and the First Companions wondered how the Society would maintain itself in the future. How will this least Society, which, however, they were certain had been formed by God, be able to grow and develop? It is still wise to pose this question in our own day: How can anyone be confident of the future of the Society of Jesus or of any religious order, for that matter? Is it not the height of naïveté or at least presumption to speak confidently about the perseverance of any individual in his vocation, let alone the continued existence of a religious order? But the bold response of the Constitutions originates in the lived experience of Ignatius and his companions: "The Society was not instituted by human means . . . but through the grace of the omnipotent hand of Christ our God and Lord. Therefore, in him alone . . . must we place our hope" (812). This is the jumping-off point for Part X, whose development is based on this fundamental conviction and on what will flow from it in the future.

To Live Out a Fundamental Choice (812)

Christ remains always the founder and the foundation of the Society (812:2)

The Society is grounded, rooted, in a special intervention by God in human history. Christ himself chose the First Companions and brought them together (see the "Deliberation of the First Fathers"). The Society continues to exist first and foremost because Christ chooses and calls each companion. The whole journey of Ignatius and the First Companions clearly shows this. *From the very beginning* in Paris through Montmartre, Venice, La Storta, and Rome, the companions were firmly convinced that they had been gathered together and were being led by God. Nadal wrote of Ignatius what he might also have written about the other companions, "[H]e was led gently he knew not where." This goes on *even now*. Christ is now and forever the head of the Society. He continues to be its founder and to found it now. It is, after all, the Society of Jesus. And in order to be more certain of responding to the Spirit, the entire Society and each of its professed members take a vow of obedience to the Vicar of Christ with respect to the missions. Development *in the future* will take place by the grace of Christ, who continues to select and call each of us and the entire body of the Society, just as he calls new companions. We are totally dependent on this call. He alone chooses us, binds us together, and sends us out. It is therefore impossible to foresee the future unless our way of foreseeing it is to place our hope in him alone and to take the means to achieve this.

Hope in him alone (812:3)

That is our response to Christ's choice of us. We speak here of a choice, a fundamental option that is always ongoing. It entails an original manner by which the entire group and each of its members maintain their special relationship with Christ. There is a radical availability leading us to abandon ourselves to him in order to be sent by him individually and corporately. We cannot base the Society on human means or our own creativity or our individual projects, but only on this hope in him alone.

This confidence in Christ alone is a crimson thread that runs through the *Pilgrim's Testament* from beginning to end and is evident throughout the life and apostolic activity of Ignatius and the early companions.[2] Hardly surprising, then, given that the Constitutions, based as they are on their own experience and designed to communicate that experience to generations to come, return time and again to this fundamental viewpoint. We have only to recall the experience of the pilgrimage (67), the preparation for the profession (82), the Preamble (134:2), the poverty of the houses (555), and the manner of accepting a mission (609–10). In every situation, it is a matter of acting on this hope in Christ alone.

> Here the Constitutions lead us back to the very source from which all things sprang. How can we doubt that our perseverance and our increase, both individual and corporate, are owing to grace? We are urged to cultivate this hope, to face the future with full confidence, provided that we actually experience Jesus as the "hidden treasure," as the reason and purpose of our existence.[3]

For this to happen, we must employ the means and specify more exactly the criteria and discernment appropriate to our life and our apostolic work.

---

[2] *PilgTest* 35–36, 40, 43, 60, 79. Also see André Ravier, "Au Gré de Dieu" and "Verbi Dei Energeia," in *Ignatius*, 358–72 and 347–55 respectively.

[3] E. Royon, in Arzubialde, *Constituciones de la Compañía*, 339.

"The first and most appropriate means": prayer and living the Eucharist (812:4)

This first means is unique and qualitatively different from all the others, including the other spiritual means (813). By placing it in no. 812, Ignatius connects it directly and immediately to hope in Christ alone. For this fundamental election fully draws us within the paschal mystery of Christ, who gives his life and who takes us with him in the work of the Father. (Recall La Storta, where Ignatius is placed with Christ carrying the cross.) This plainly signifies that the Society is brought into the mystery of the Eucharistic Christ. In this light we penetrate the deeper meaning of no. 812:4 and the seriousness of its language: "In conformity with this hope . . . prayers and Masses will be offered for this holy intention." The daily Eucharist expresses the essential conviction of union with the Eucharistic mystery of Christ himself. Hence the profound importance of daily Mass in our life, as Fr. General has often reminded us. Those Masses that we are urged to celebrate monthly for the Church, the Society, the intentions of Fr. General, our benefactors, and deceased Jesuits give concrete expression to this mystery in our existence.

Other Means toward Living This Election (813–815)

The spiritual means (813)

How do we effectively carry out in our practical daily lives this fundamental election of "hope in him alone"? Here again we encounter the dynamic of the Incarnation so characteristic of the Ignatian approach. "All good things and all the gifts descend from on high" (*SpEx* 237), coming from Christ our Lord. Since the purpose of the Society is "to help souls to attain their supreme goal," the companions should be "instruments closely united with God, allowing themselves to be led by the divine hand," and this disposition should be externalized by the spiritual means specified in no. 813. These means are more efficacious than those calculated to win the esteem of others. Ignatius insists that priority be given to solid virtues and to spiritual matters (813:4). These interior gifts are the ones that will render the outward ones more genuine and effective in attaining the goal to be sought (813:5). For Ignatius, these apparently quite personal actions not only contribute to the spiritual life of the individual but also condition and foster the apostolic productivity of the Society as a whole.

The human means (814)

The Ignatian movement descending from above (812) to what is below leads us along an incarnational path whereby the instrument of the Lord (813) is equipped with the human means necessary to encounter his contemporaries (814). Hence follows the importance of attentively cultivating human gifts, specifically through the studies addressed in Part IV, "not that we place our trust in them, but rather that we cooperate with God's grace." At this point we are touching upon a key principle of Ignatian spirituality: "to seek and find God in all things." And this principle itself is rooted in the spiritual experience at the Cardoner (*PilgTest* 29), an experience that the one making the Spiritual Exercises is asked to relive during the Contemplation for Obtaining Love (*SpEx* 231–37).

A few years had to elapse before Ignatius could assimilate this paradox and place all his confidence in God alone while integrating the human means as well. At the time of his pilgrimage to the Holy Land after his conversion, he did in fact try to avoid all human means (money, food, companionship) in order to rely entirely on God alone (*PilgTest* 35, 36). Gradually, he learned to live out the paradox. It was not at first a result of intellectual comprehension but more a question of living existentially. This explains why he will wish young Jesuits during their years of formation to put into practice themselves this hope in God without the help of human means, by immersing themselves in the limitations of the human lot, such as those proposed in the experiences (64–69). Gradually this reliance on God alone is called on to embody itself and find its concrete expression by integration with human means such as education, institutional structures, and the equipment necessary for effective work. So, grant that one could say of the Jesuit that, all other things being equal, he shows more reliance on God alone while employing human means than while doing without them. But what is important here is to use human means in such a way as to make using them a veritable sacrament or outward sign of this hope in God alone. There is, of course, a way of using them that might instead undermine the Society because it attacks this basic principle. This is true whether we place our entire confidence in them, or forget that in using these human means we must always remain docile instruments in the hands of the Lord. Integrating human means with reliance on God alone is a never ending challenge to the individual Jesuit and to the Society at large. While using these necessary human aids, do we preserve our heart free and available, "for your love and your grace are enough for me"?

The institutional means (815)

As we mentioned earlier while analyzing the structure of Part X, Ignatius moved this paragraph from its original position following no. 818 (dealing with ambition) to place it in its present position just after no. 814, the discussion of human means. Furthermore, he connected the two by means of the adverb *equally* at the beginning of no. 815. Seemingly, one can perceive an obvious extension of the Incarnational logic at play here. The gift of God in Christ goes so far as to embody itself within the very human means, namely, the colleges and also the universities. These are understood both as Gospel-inspired educational enterprises and as "seminaries" or "nurseries" for the Society. While not speaking directly of ecclesiastical seminaries, Ignatius does envision the colleges as grounding a human and Christian hope that they could result in "vocations to the Society." In these institutions he recognized the potential for increasing and renewing the Society. It would be quite difficult, therefore, for the Society to do without these institutions if it wishes to renew itself in accordance with God's will.

The Internal Life of the Society (816–822)

Having presented the attitude and the means essential to the maintenance and growth of the group, the text proceeds to a discussion of other measures and other criteria for discernment that are also important and likely to be helpful. These will pertain both to the internal life of the Society and to its life of apostolic action. Although they were already treated with some care in earlier Parts of the Constitutions, Ignatius had learned from experience that these policies were of pivotal importance to sustaining a lively hope in Christ alone.

With regard to the internal life of the Society, the *first two means* mentioned have to do with *poverty* (816) and the path of *humility,* so fundamental to our vocation (817–18). It is illuminating to realize that we are being drawn back both individually and as a group to the fundamental requirements of our vocation to follow the humble and poor Christ. Here we recall the colloquy of the Two Standards, where we pray "that we might obtain the grace to be received under the banner of Christ in poverty . . . and in humiliations (*SpEx* 146–47). For Ignatius hopes that each of his companions "accepts and desires with all possible energy whatever Christ our Lord has loved and embraced" (101).

While studying chapter 2 of Part VI, concerning poverty, we have already noted that Ignatius regarded the acceptance of fixed revenues as a major obstacle to hope in Christ alone. It was his experience and that of his first companions.[4] In the same way, the acceptance of ecclesiastical dignities, so closely intertwined with ambition, would draw us away from our companionship with Christ on the path of humility. It is worthwhile indeed to read the correspondence of Ignatius and ponder the steps he took to head off the nomination of several companions as bishops, namely, Le Jay, Bobadilla, Laínez, Broët, Canisius, and Borgia. On the other hand, it was he who asked Frs. Barreto, Oviedo, and Carneiro to accept episcopal consecration in order to undertake a dangerous and difficult mission in Ethiopia. These three priests were, in fact, the reason for the fifth simple vow of the professed; they were anxious to remain in close contact with Ignatius even though no longer under obedience to him.

We might marvel that Ignatius prescribes the four simple vows having to do with ambition (817). Here we have clear sign of the importance that he attached to this matter. As in the case of the simple vow of poverty related to the solemn vow of poverty in Part VI (553), this spells out a way of trusting in God, that he will protect us from ambition and accom-

---

[4] Recall his lengthy discernment on the poverty of the churches, recorded in the *Spiritual Journal.*

plish in us what might not be possible if we are left to our own human weakness.

GC 34 reaffirmed the desire of the Society to resist episcopal appointments not only to maintain our total availability for missions, but also to remain "this least Society of Jesus."[5] The Complementary Norms, on the other hand, specify the procedures to be followed should a Jesuit be asked by the Holy See to shoulder the duties of a bishop (*CN* 139, §3)

A *third means* concerns the *preservation in good condition of the body of Society*, always to be safeguarded with great care (819–22). These paragraphs hark back to some key points already developed in Parts I, II, III, V, VI, VIII, and IX. Noteworthy also is the *wise moderation* or "mediocridad" to be preserved in the Constitutions, which allow us to temper a *magis* marked by too little discernment.

The Apostolic Life of the Society (823–827)

Finally in these last paragraphs, the Constitutions offer some cautions regarding human and institutional means (814–15) These wise counsels, seemingly secondary, indicate "the way of proceeding" employed by Ignatius and the First Companions in approaching their apostolic work: "a universal love which includes in our Lord all parties . . . along with care in preserving the goodwill and friendship of all, so that God our Lord might be better served and glorified in all things" (823–24). At the same time, they reflect a concern for the truth and modesty that should characterize each Jesuit's activities and presentation of himself, not displaying his privileges; this will increase the devotion of others, and also allow for mutual assistance toward the attainment of a common purpose (825). Universal love and personal modesty—these are traits typical of men whose hearts are burning to proclaim Jesus Christ and his Gospel. These are attitudes rooted in reliance on him alone. And "to serve the Lord alone" always included for Ignatius service to "the Church his spouse under the Roman Pontiff, the Vicar of Christ on earth" (*FI* 1). The reference to the Apostolic See recurs twice in these paragraphs (824 and 825). It is a

---

[5] *Thirty-Fourth General Congregation*, d. 6, no. 193 (pp. 98–99).

subtle reminder of their attachment to the Vicar of Christ to whom they have pledged themselves and who is always the one who ultimately sends them forth in the name of Christ.

The last two paragraphs point up well the practical realism of St. Ignatius: the health of each member, the monthly reading of the important passages in the Constitutions, and finally, the location of houses in a healthful environment where the air is good (826–27). Far from ending on a solemn note, the Constitutions conclude with an eye to ecology.

OPEN TO THE FUTURE:
THE COMPLEMENTARY NORMS

Ignatius never finished the Constitutions. This incompleteness was not accidental. Of course, one might easily think otherwise, since he died before concluding Part IV. But a reading of Part X shows unmistakably that, far from wishing to conclude the Constitutions, he chose to leave them open to the future. This openness is faithful to the dynamic that pervades the entire work. It is an organic and progressive dynamic, not aimed from the very first at prescribing what must be done, but rather at establishing criteria for discernment that will "aid us to proceed better, in conformity with our Institute, along the path of divine service on which we have entered" (134). This will permit us to make the necessary elections and decisions in an almost infinite variety of historical, social, and cultural situations as they arise during different times, in different places, and amid different civilizations. This openness can also be detected in certain verbal clues strategically placed throughout this entire work. Examples of these are the frequent (165 times) use of the verb *convenir* in Spanish (*convenire* in Latin), which means "to suit, to be appropriate, convenient, or agreeable," along with the recurrence of expressions like "as far as possible," "whenever possible," "as much as possible." Add to this the unflagging attention to circumstances and the strong support given to subsidiarity.[1]

The Constitutions were born out of the experience of Ignatius and his companions, subjected to prayerful discern-

---

[1] These thoughts took their inspiration from the excellent article by Ignacio Iglesias that we have cited earlier in this work, "Constitutiones para hacer Constitutiones." Unless otherwise noted, quotations in this chapter are drawn from Fr. Iglesias's article.

ment. And the experience of living the Constitutions will, in turn, show that they are a text deliberately left unfinished, calling out to be completed and further enriched, starting from a lived experience that is ever new. They challenge us "not only to walk along the road that the 'First Companions of the Society' (53, 81) have laid out and that we are committed to following. They also indicate the way we should move forward and continue to explore and discover them anew." They have recourse, therefore, to other texts that will likewise be born of experience lived and prayerfully discerned at a given moment in history. At the dawn of the third millennium, the Thirty-fourth General Congregation gave concrete expression to creative fidelity to the Constitutions as lived by the companions in the present situation of the Church and the world. This fidelity will never be fully achieved by men marching along on the "path toward him," (*FI 1*), which we know as the Society of Jesus. "Thus we now have our updated travel manual, which is the *Constitutions of the Society of Jesus and Their Complementary Norms*, a book that is an indivisible whole."

The Complementary Norms are in effect "the sign and the result of the Society's creative fidelity to the vital dynamism of the Constitutions and to the intention of St. Ignatius not to conclude them."[2] The Constitutions cannot be read except in reference to the Norms, which require the former in order to remain alive in the here and now. The Norms, for their part, must not be understood as fully completed, but as the most recent expression of a process that is always open to further cooperation with the work of the Lord that is the Constitutions. Our pilgrimage is carried on in accordance with a "dynamic of the provisional." "Our responsibility toward the Norms is not only to observe them as an extension of the Constitutions, but also to learn continually from living them, as

---

[2] Ibid., 170. This creative fidelity as expressed in the Norms first of all manifests itself in the priorities set up by the Society for the choice of its missions, but also in many other aspects of our life in companionship. Fr. Iglesias cites four of these: chastity, poverty, collaboration with the laity, and also the community. Strangely enough, the Norms have nothing to say about this last-mentioned priority, but Fr. Kolvenbach has forcefully recalled it to our attention.

happens when we allow ourselves to be guided by God through the very history we ourselves produce by our creative fidelity to living them."

Cooperation with the action of Christ as he continues to found the Society (134, 812, 813) is described by Ignatius as "involving the rhythm of my own inner being through two actions essential to our way of proceeding and expressed in two words, *sentir* and *accomplir*; that is, 'to feel, to understand' what God wants and 'to accomplish' what we have thus experienced. In this way we realize the cooperation that God asks of his creatures, the 'desiring and choosing only that which is more conducive' called for in the Principle and Foundation" (*SpEx* 23). We always return to the mystical roots of the Constitutions as they were lived in the *Spiritual Journal*, recording Ignatius's interior movements, and recounted in the *Pilgrim's Testament* (*PilgTest* 99–101).

It is in this light that we can understand how to observe the Constitutions (602) properly and completely, as Ignatius hoped. For him it was not a matter of simply applying rules and regulations. Rather it was a question of gazing upward, of looking toward God our Lord at work (*SpEx* 236), and viewing each concrete situation in the light of the Gospels, with the aid of the criteria furnished by the Constitutions and the Norms. It will always be possible not only to discern and sense what God wills but also to test it and to accomplish it.

Applied in this way, the Constitutions with the Norms will help us go as far as the First Companions and even further in the Lord (81).

BIBLIOGRAPHY

PRIMARY SOURCES

The Constitutions of the Society of Jesus and Their Complementary Norms. St. Louis: Institute of Jesuit Sources, 1996.

Documents of the 31st and 32nd General Congregations of the Society of Jesus. St. Louis: Institute of Jesuit Sources, 1977.

The Documents of Vatican II. Edited by Walter M. Abbott, S.J. New York: Guild Press, America Press, Association Press, 1966.

Documents of the Thirty-Fourth General Congregation of the Society of Jesus. St. Louis: Institute of Jesuit Sources, 1995.

"Exposcit debitum." In *The Constitutions of the Society of Jesus and Their Complementary Norms.*

Ignatius of Loyola. *Journal spirituel.* Translated into French by Maurice Giuliani, S.J., with a commentary. Christus Collection, no. 1. Paris: Desclée de Brouwer, 1959.

"Lumen gentium." In *The Documents of Vatican II.*

Monumenta Constitutionum prævia. Vol. 1 of *Sancti Ignatii de Loyola Constitutiones Societatis Iesu,* Monumenta Ignatiana, ser. 3; vol. 63 of Monumenta historica Societatis Iesu. Rome, 1934.

A Pilgrim's Testament: Memoirs of St. Ignatius of Loyola. Translated by Parmanandra R. Divarkar, S.J. St. Louis: Institute of Jesuit Sources, 1995.

"Regimini militantis Ecclesiæ." In *The Constitutions of the Society of Jesus and Their Complementary Norms.*

The Spiritual Exercises of Saint Ignatius. Translation and commentary by George E Ganss, S.J. St. Louis: The Institute of Jesuit Sources, 1992.

The Spiritual Journal of St. Ignatius Loyola. Translated by William J. Young, S.J. Woodstock, Md., 1958.

Secondary Sources

Books Cited

Arzubialde, S., ed. *Constituciones de la Compañía de Jesús*. Bilbao: Mensajero-Sal Terrae, 1994.

Bertrand, Dominique. *Un Corps pour l'Esprit: Essai sur les Constitutions*. Christus Collection, no. 38. Paris: Desclée de Brouwer, 1974.

————. *La Politique de saint Ignace de Loyola*. Paris: Cerf, 1985.

Costa, M., S.J. *Legge religiosa e discernimento spirituale nelle Constituzione della Compagnía di Gesù*. Brescia, 1973.

Decloux, Simon, S.J. *La Voie ignatienne*. Paris: DDB, 1983.

Eliot, T. S. "Little Gidding," *Four Quartets*. London: Faber andf Faber, 1945.

Favre, Pierre, S.J. *The Spiritual Writings of Pierre Favre: The* Memoriale *and Selected Letters and Instructions*. Translated by Edmond C. Murphy, S.J. St. Louis: Institute of Jesuit Sources, 1996.

Giuliani, Maurice, S.J., et al., eds. and trans. *Écrits*. Collection Christus, no. 76. Paris: Desclée de Brouwer, 1991.

Gonçalves da Câmara, Luis, S.J. *Le Récit du pélerin: Autobiographie de saint Ignace de Loyola*. Translated into French by A. Lauras, notes by J.-Cl. Dhôtel. Christus Collection. Paris: Desclée de Brouwer, 1988.

Iglesias, Ignacio. "Sexta Parte, Introduccion." In Arzubialde, *Constituciones de la Compañía de Jesús*.

Kolvenbach, Peter-Hans, S.J. Introductory Discourses, no. 3: "On Our Law and Our Life." In *Documents of the Thirty-Fourth General Congregation of the Society of Jesus*.

Our Jesuit Life. St. Louis: Institute of Jesuit Sources, 1990.

"P. Hieronymi Nadal Exhortationes in Hispania, 1554." In *Fontes narrativi de S. Ignatio de Loyola et de Societatis Iesu initiis*, vol. 1, ed. Dionysius Fernandez Zapico and Candidus de Dalmases; vol. 55 of Monumenta historica Societatis Iesu. Rome, 1943.

Polanco, Juan de, S.J. *Epistolæ et commentaria*, 726–807. Vol. 2 of *Polanci complementa;* vol. 54 of Monumenta historica Societatis Iesu. Madrid, 1917.

Rahner, Hugo, S.J. *Ignatius of Loyola: Letters to Women*. Translated from the original German *Ignatius von Loyola: Briefwechsel mit Frauen* by Kathleen Pond and S. A. H. Weetman. New York: Herder and Herder, 1960.

Ravier, André. *Ignatius of Loyola and the Founding of the Society of Jesus*. San Francisco: Ignatius Press, 1987.

Soltero, Carlos, S.J. In Calvez, *Incorporation of a Spirit*, 225–52.

Articles Cited

Aldama, Antonio de, S.J. "De coadjutoribus Societatis Jesu in mente et in praxi Sancti Ignatii." *Archivum historicum Societatis Iesu* 38 (1969): 389–430.

Bertrand, Dominique. "Un Mariage avec la culture." *Christus*, no. 117 (Jan. 1983): 105–9.

Buckley, Michael J., S.J. "Final Vows: Culmination of an Ignatian Election." *National Jesuit News*, April 1981, 8 and 10.

Calvez, J.-Y., S.J., et al. *Constitutions of the Society of Jesus: Incorporation of a Spirit. CIS*, 1993.

Chapelle, A. "Le Quatrième Voeu dans la Compagnie. *CIS*, 1978.

Corella, Jesus. "La Genèse de l'idée de mission chez Ignace de Loyola: De l'appel à aider les âmes à la rédaction des *Constitutions.*" *CIS*, no. 72 (1933, 1): 9–26.

Decloux, Simon, S.J. Chapter in *Constitutions of the Society of Jesus: Incorporation of a Spirit*. Rome: CIS, 1993.

Dezza, Paulo, S.J. "The Members of the Society." In *The Formula of the Institute*. Rome: CIS, 1982.

Hausmann, Noelle. "Pour La Profession super hostiam: Une étude de la profession religieuse." *Nouvelle Revue Théologique* 110 (1988): 729–42.

———. "Une Lecture du *Journal spirituel.*" *CIS* (1990), nos. 63–64 (pp. 38–57).

Iglesias, Ignacio, S.J. "Constitutiones para hacer Constitutiones." *Manresa* 70 (1997): 165–69.

Kolvenbach, Peter-Hans, S.J. Letter "On the 450th Anniversary of the Vows of Montmartre." *Acta Romana* 19, no. 1 (1988): 80–83.

———. "Some Aspects of Formation: From the End of the Novitiate to the Beginning of Regency." *Acta Romana* 20, no. 1 (1988): 85–106.

———. "On the State of the Society." *Acta Romana* 20, no. 3 (1990): 484.

———. Letter. *Acta Romana* 21, no. 1 (1994): 52–53.

———. "La vocation et la mission du frère Jésuite." *CIS* 78 (1995): 13.

Lukács, Ladislas. "De graduum diverstate inter sacerdotes in Societate Iesu." *Archivum historicum Societatis Iesu* 36 (1968): 237–316.

Rendina, S. "La Pauvreté' de la Compagnie, *CIS*, no. 3 (1993): 55–74.

Royon, E. "Être mis, par le Père, avec le Christ évangélisateur." *CIS*, no. 86 (1997, 3): 60–80.